HybridP3M

HybridP3M

Processes in Optimized, Mature Environments

Lukasz Rosinski

BEP

BUSINESS EXPERT PRESS

Leader in applied, concise business books

First published in 2021 by
Business Expert Press, LLC
222 East 46th Street, New York, NY 10017
www.businessexpertpress.com

ISBN-13: 978-1-63742-088-1 (paperback)
ISBN-13: 978-1-63742-089-8 (e-book)

Business Expert Press Portfolio and Project Management Collection

Collection ISSN: 2156-8189 (print)
Collection ISSN: 2156-8200 (electronic)

First edition: 2021

10 9 8 7 6 5 4 3 2 1

Description

Hybrid P3M: Processes in Optimized, Mature Environments is an advanced technical book for hybrid project and program management. It is a complete methodology covering both processes as well as principles, according to a sound meta-model. Essentially, it combines the benefits of predictive and agile delivery and it aligns with the Projects with Learning Outcomes (ProwLO) methodology introduced in *Knowledge Management for Project Excellence*, by Lukasz Rosinski.

It also aligns with the PRINCE2 method, and provides an alternative for PRINCE2-Agile, combining traditional control and flexible agile traditions. It is a *holistic* method, addressing Project, Program, Portfolio Management (P3M) interfaces and topics such as leadership. Based on HybridP3M's process model, derived from common enterprise project functions (such as project planning) functional achievement is recommended and feasible.

Each HybridP3M process is analyzed according to unique process aspects. Furthermore, a new maturity framework is introduced called MAIDEO. At the end of every process Chapter requirements are provided for different maturity levels. The specific benefits of the HybridP3M methodology include:

- eases the burden on project managers thanks to joint process responsibility,
- controlled environments thanks to traditional management,
- change responsive agile delivery process,
- pathway to optimized and mature organizations,
- functional P3M achievement thanks to functional processes

Keywords

hybrid method; hybrid project management; holistic; leadership; matrix approach; P3M interfaces; functional achievement; integrating knowledge management; knowmadic-steps technique; predictive delivery model; agile delivery model; agile product delivery process; complements ProwLO; Projects with Learning Outcomes; MAIDEO requirements; Maturity Alignment In Dimension of Enterprise Origin; cases-method

Contents

Acknowledgments

The author would like to thank Douglas Weidner and Mary McKinlay for their peer review in the publishing process. Their feedback resulted in a few modifications and improvements of the manuscript. These improvements were added to the introduction. Also thank you to Adam Swallow, editor at the Oxford University Press, whose feedback on my book proposal and the project motivated me to continue. The author quotes: "I think the whole project is shaping up to be a fascinating and wonderful resource. It should, if developed, managed, and published in the right way, make a significant contribution to the community it seeks to engage." In the context of the publication and editing process, the author would like to thank Tim Kloppenborg and Kam Jugdev for their general approval and their inspirational, constructive feedback on the draft manuscript. Thanks to their comments, the manuscript was restructured and much better organized. Finally, the author would like to thank Scott Isenberg for the opportunity to get this book published in a very competitive market. There are many "methods" out there claiming best practice.

Introduction

Since the advent of the Agile paradigm, traditional project management is often interpreted as a waterfall approach to projects. The popular discussion on this subject is mainly about the differences between these two models. Many subject matter experts have correctly noted however that Agile (taking into account every single Agile approach on the market) is not a project management method. Instead, it is an umbrella concept for Agile Product Delivery, a subfunction of projects. Project management, on the other hand, is at a higher level, also a subfunction of projects. So the discussion should be strictly on the delivery model: Agile or waterfall. But the key question is: given the fundamental delivery model, what is the best management approach for projects? Depending on the industry, the most dominant delivery model could be Agile. While infrastructure projects in the construction industry tend to be organized in linear sequential phases (similar to waterfall), other industries increasingly are adopting Agile methods. Agile is most popular in IT for software development. Another trend on the rise is the hybrid model, blending traditional project management with Agile. The latter indicates that Agile has limitations with regard to project management, which is another discussion, only partly related to the delivery model. It should be noted that the chosen delivery model has an impact on the management requirements for a successful delivery. In other words, the delivery model partly shapes the management environment as institutionalized by an adopted method.

The HybridP3M method, introduced in this book, acknowledges the importance of Agile for successful projects. The ability to respond quickly to changes, a key Agile proposition, is simply a key requirement of business in the twenty-first century. In the context of projects, being agile implies being responsive to change during a project, mainly based on changing requirements. Agility at the organizational level, like dealing with a portfolio of projects and programs, is not the focus of this book. Following the Agile premise, HybridP3M has adopted Agile Product Delivery as one of its processes. However, in HybridP3M, Agile Product

Delivery, as a process and as part of a wider framework, is essentially a trade-off and not restricted to an Agile delivery method (if selected at the expense of predictive delivery). Besides the delivery method, an agile "qualification" for product delivery may depend on other factors as well (e.g., mindset, culture in general). Furthermore, Agile Product Delivery may imply Agile project management in general (with specific implications for higher-level processes and P3M interfaces), making the popular discussion on Agile complicated and diverse. More specifically, agility is a continuum of management overhead (for the benefit of greater control) and flexible delivery (for the benefit of greater customer satisfaction) as opposites. In other words, although Agile Product Delivery strongly correlates with an Agile delivery mode, the notion of Agile has greater meaning and should be analyzed in the context of enterprise-wide project management, at a higher level, in order to better understand the concept of Agile project management, as opposed to traditional management (without hybrid elements). This flexible approach characterized by a trade-off means that HybridP3M is a generic project management method. Depending on the industry and type of project, including the delivery model, agility is a variable.

The intended audience for this book includes project management team members who seek a robust project management methodology that combines the benefits of predictive and agile methods. The defined processes consist of subactivities that need to be executed for functional achievement (to do what is required in different process areas and, thus, knowledge areas). Functional achievement based on optimized processes is the main goal for project teams. Project or program success depends on it to a very high degree. In other words, functional achievement is a critical success factor for successful projects/programs. Second, business owners/senior responsible owners (who are engaged in portfolios, programs, projects), enterprise architects, process managers, and project management officers are targeted because they play a key role in the process of institutionalizing hybrid project management (the main thesis of this work), as well as drive the maturity levels of the project management function and related P3M functions (reflecting an interconnected organizational system interfacing with projects/programs, which highly depends on knowledge about projects).

It is an advantage that the reader has advanced knowledge about PRINCE2, a traditional process-based method, or is familiar with the Praxis Framework, launched by Adrian Dooley, which provides a free resource online (https://praxisframework.org). The methodology in this book is inspired by the scientific approach of method engineering. This means that it is not an easy how-to guide. Luckily, not all complex processes, the bulk of the methodology, need to be mastered by one single person, depending on his or her role in the project. Every specific role should focus on a particular knowledge area. This is referred to as joint responsibility for project management. Familiarity with "Projects with Learning Outcomes" (ProwLO), a methodology introduced in *Knowledge Management for Project Excellence* (Rosinski 2019), is also important. This Project Knowledge Management (PKM) methodology is used in one of the processes and plays a key role in advancing enterprise maturity levels (for the sake of optimization).

HybridP3M is positioning itself as a P3M (Project, Program, Portfolio Management)-integrated discipline, not just plain project management. The Praxis framework was the first approach to notice that the distinction between projects and programs is artificial. It is rather a continuum. Also, the notion that programs are collections of projects is not always the case. Think of change initiatives managed as programs. Accordingly, the management of projects and programs follows the same processes and principles. Another factor is the fact that there are many interfaces between different functions. In other words, projects and programs are interlinked with the rest of an organization, in particular the portfolio management function. In this book, the term projects can be interchanged with programs on many occasions.

As compared to other existing methods, HybridP3M's closest competitor is PRINCE2 Agile, owned by AXELOS. This method combines PRINCE2, a traditional approach based on an extensive process model, with Agile submethods such as Scrum. According to this approach, Agile methods are compatible with an overarching PRINCE2 framework. With regard to the PRINCE2 part, there are few changes as compared to the original PRINCE2 method. HybridP3M, on the other hand, has built a traditional framework from scratch and embedded Agile in a multidimensional way (e.g., through principles and processes). Based on the notion of a project approach combining flexible delivery mode (essentially a binary option between predictive and Agile) and generic processes, HybridP3M is applicable across many different project types. However, its Agile Product Delivery process is most suitable for projects focused on systems engineering. Civil engineering disciplines, characterized by predictive deliveries organized around Work Packages, may benefit from HybridP3M as well, but industry-wide Agile delivery is becoming more dominant, and therefore, HybridP3M focuses on Agile product delivery. The latter process is shaped by an Agile delivery mode (as opposed to predictive), transforming the delivery process across industries, following early success in software development.

What makes HybridP3M stand out is the characteristic threefold matrix model of the method. Borrowed from Agile tradition, project management roles and responsibilities are distributed among the team. Accordingly, HybridP3M assumes that project management is a joint effort, performed by multiple actors. This approach results in a matrix. In fact, depending on the viewpoint, there are three 2-dimensional matrices. The first matrix relates project roles to HybridP3M's processes. The second matrix relates individuals with a specific role to real projects given a portfolio. So the first matrix is at the project/program level, while the second matrix is at the portfolio level. The first matrix is an essential part of project management according to HybridP3M, whereas the second matrix can be used for capacity planning in the context of portfolio management. The third matrix relates HybridP3M processes with high-level PRINCE2 processes—not the prescriptive, detailed activities of the latter. Adopting PRINCE2 processes is important when adopting the ProwLO methodology for project knowledge management, a parallel process model to PRINCE2 based on a project's life cycle. For example, the HybridP3M process of evaluating a project relates to the PRINCE2 processes of managing stage boundaries (SB) and closing a project (CP). SB provides an opportunity for gate reviews, whereas CP provides an opportunity for end-of-project reviews (also known as postcontrol). So at a high level, PRINCE2 is compatible with HybridP3M. But HybridP3M differs from PRINCE2 fundamentally as it has a completely different process model, in contrast to PRINCE2, not based on a project's life cycle depending on time.

HybridP3M's processes are derived from functions. Functions exist in every organization. They are specializations part of a value or supply chain. Based on functions it is possible to define roles and responsibilities and, later on, assign people to perform related tasks. Functions also drive processes, not the other way around. Processes have process goals to transform the state of something based on activity, whereas functions have objectives providing reason to engage in an activity in the first place and a value proposition to justify allocation of human resources. Unlike lifecycle-based process models embedded in PRINCE2 or Praxis, Hybrid-P3M's process model does not correspond to predetermined time bands, unless compensated by a matrix that relates HybridP3M's processes that way, effectively *extending* the process model. This does not mean that all of HybridP3M's processes are continuous, from the beginning to the end of a project. It means that project management processes as defined by HybridP3M should not be dictated by time. The underlying assumption is that activity typical for a specific process is difficult to predict in terms of when it is triggered as a project unfolds. In other words, HybridP3M claims that activity occurs relatively chaotically based on project dynamics (which are usually not linear, even disregarding the delivery model). On top of that, besides poor time triggers, activity triggers due to events are also questionable. A project management process, not automated by Artificial Intelligence, is still subject to the interpretation of an actor who may initiate specific activity or not, and different people react to events differently for various reasons (like process understanding). This shift away from a rigid process model enables HybridP3M to create an opportunity for Agile project management, not just product delivery. In any way, HybridP3M is not an advocate of bureaucratic project management, a common perception of existing bodies of knowledge and methodologies fueling the popularity of Agile.

HybridP3M goes beyond process-based project management and calls for knowledge-based project management (Gasik 2007), as an additional principle. The main weakness of process-based approaches, which are dominating the market, is that they overestimate how manageable projects are. They provide a step-by-step guide as a recipe for success. While procedures may be useful in some cases, reality is much more complex. One of the key problems these methods are dealing with in practice is that projects differ in nature, making a one-size-fits-all solution impossible. Across industries and within, there are many types of projects. While you may categorize them according to size, complexity, risk, and industry-specific characteristics, it is a mystique to scale or tailor methods using such parameters. This mystique is rooted in the claim of generic applicability as bodies of knowledge are often marketed that way (with zealous consequences by convinced followers). But in practice, scaling and tailoring is questionable as there is no reason to assume it is common, even with access to tailoring or scaling guidelines. That said, evidence of tailoring/scaling (both imply changes in process) can be found. For example, some organizations have a policy to perform a project evaluation only when the budget is beyond a certain limit. From a method owner's perspective, tailoring or perhaps scaling (less rigorous modification) is clever if owners want to maintain claims of generic applicability, but, nonetheless, it only complicates the matter and certainly is not elegant. From a user's perspective, tailoring only makes sense, arguably, if it is a one-time investment in order to develop a custom-built methodology that can be used organization-wide. The alternative is to accept project diversity and the limitations of process models. Instead, why not create a less-prescriptive, downsized (look at how complex *PMBoK*, 5th and 6th editions, is—see Project Management Institute 2013 and 2017 respectively), back-to-the-essence process and complement it with the notion that project members should have access to actionable knowledge that they can apply in projects? This is the kind of knowledge-based project management HybridP3M advocates. Finally, knowledge-based project management is a progressive approach. The more knowledge can be accumulated, the better. Potentially there is no limit, and therefore any guide is too limited. Personal knowledge mastery is therefore a driving force.

Maturity is an important theme in HybridP3M. The term "mature environments" refers to a situation where projects are governed by mature organizations. The organizational context or cross-organizational context with all stakeholders sets the conditions for effective project management. Organizational maturity shapes the project environment, which should be treated as a given, and will have an impact on project success. HybridP3M intends to challenge the isolationist view on project management of standalone projects, as imposed by, for example, PRINCE2. Taking into account the importance of maturity levels, HybridP3M introduces MAIDEO (Maturity Alignment in Dimensions of Enterprise Origin), a companion maturity model. Generally, maturity can be measured at the level of functions, including subfunctions of functions. Projects consisting of subfunctions like project management, product delivery management, project knowledge management, and project direction have maturity levels most critical to project success. Project success furthermore depends on the maturity levels of other functions that play a role in the overall project or portfolio management process (across projects). Based on existing evidence of interfaces resulting from interlinked functions, characterized by information or product flows, it follows that project management is definitely not an isolated phenomenon. Projects are much more integrated with other organizational functions as previously addressed. In conclusion, HybridP3M is ambitious. This method is founded on the hope that organizations are willing to invest in maturity, not just for the sake of project management success but for business in general.

There is a need for a consistent, coherent, and comprehensive methodology for hybrid project management. In the current situation, a hybrid approach, combining predictive and Agile elements, is highly in demand, a trend on the rise. But so far, no method has been developed (as-is), with the exception of PRINCE2-Agile, which is remarkably silent about its hybrid dimension. In most cases, only the idea of hybrid project management is explored, based on diverse interpretations. The HybridP3M methodology ends all confusion and provides a framework that can be implemented in practice. It involves the adoption of HybridP3M principles and processes in an organizational setting, called embedding or institutionalizing. Institutionalizing HybridP3M, and thereby building hybrid capability, is the situation to-be. The biggest complication is that project team members must develop greater process awareness, not from a bureaucratic but a functional point of view. Team members should not become "slaves of the methodology," a potential pitfall of traditional methods that strongly depend on complex process models, like PRINCE2 and Praxis framework. The solution is personal knowledge mastery and knowledge-based project management, in which knowledge management plays a key role.

This book is structured in 16 chapters. The first Chapter is titled "Introduction to Processes," in which a meta-model of the methodology is presented (as the backbone of the method), process aspects are explained, and all 14 HybridP3M processes are introduced. In Chapter 2, there is a focus on method foundations such as matrices and principles. The following 14 chapters correspond to HybridP3M's processes, first introduced in Chapter 1. At the foundation of every process there is a process diagram. The graphical representation is based on a technique called Process Data Modelling (Weerd 2006), borrowed from science. These figures are called Process-Data Diagrams (PDD). On the left hand side are depicted activities (process steps) and on the right hand side the output is presented. The output side consists of (data) concepts or products. Most activities—but not all—are meant to produce or update something. Some concepts are complex and are depicted either with dark edges or as composite objects. In Appendix I, the Cases method is explained, a method that supports decision making and captures knowledge about decisions.

CHAPTER 1

Introduction to Processes

In this chapter, a meta-model is introduced that serves to better understand HybridP3M as a novel methodology. Every element of this meta-model is important. Next, process aspects are explained as to better position HybridP3M processes with some meta-data (data about processes). Then, HybridP3M's fourteen unique processes are introduced. A graphical depiction of the combined processes is missing as the processes are difficult to relate with one another (based on complex relationships, independent execution, or an extra dimension such as time in life cycle management). It is better to present a model of project enterprise functions that lays the foundation for functional processes (see Figure 1.1).

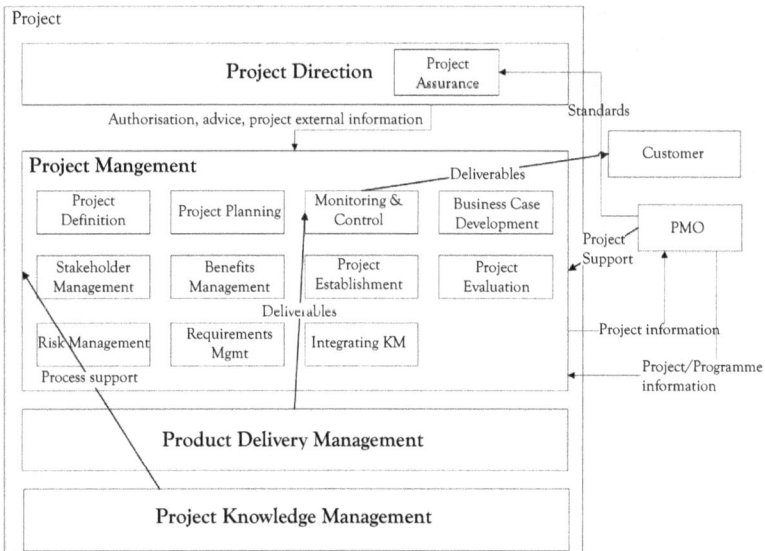

Figure 1.1 Project Enterprise Functions (adapted from Rosinski, 2019, p. 41)

Meta-model

Meta-models are important in the process of method engineering, a niche scientific discipline. The meta-model behind HybridP3M follows a generic best practice structure. The backbone of this structure consists of process, activity, role, and product. According to this structure, processes consist of one or more activities. Activities are performed by roles, and each engaging role has a specific relation to an activity. This means that if multiple roles engage in the same activity, their role in terms of action differs. Activities transform products. Products are used as input, part of the output, or being updated (implying that they have states in the context of a larger process). Roles are the first factor of activity and are based on enterprise functions, staging formal and informal positions within a (temporary) organization. The first factor refers to the fact that activities are a function of engaging roles in the context of larger processes grouping these activities when defined formally. Every distinct role has a unique approach in the context of a process, and this is evidenced by the type or way activity is performed. Then there exists a second factor, which is per definition weaker. The second factor places activities in context. Contextual understanding of activity remains a factor because it helps to define activities in the first place. Note that definition of activities is relevant in not only method engineering but also project planning, namely prior to schedule formation. The most notable candidates for the second factor are enterprise functions, perspectives or aspects, and legal ramifications (driven by project contracts). The final element of the meta-model is independent aspect characterized by indirect relationship with the other elements. So an element that does not relate to the process model itself but provides broader context for the development of a body of knowledge. And the best candidate is arguably principle. All principles combined reflect the philosophy behind a methodology. See Figure 1.2 for a graphical depiction of the meta-model based on the explained structure. Note that the concept associations have "multiplicity" (based on unified modeling language [UML] conventions).

HybridP3M consists of fourteen processes that provide the foundation of the process model. A process model is a detailed mapping of process-related elements. In case of HybridP3M, the process model relates to the

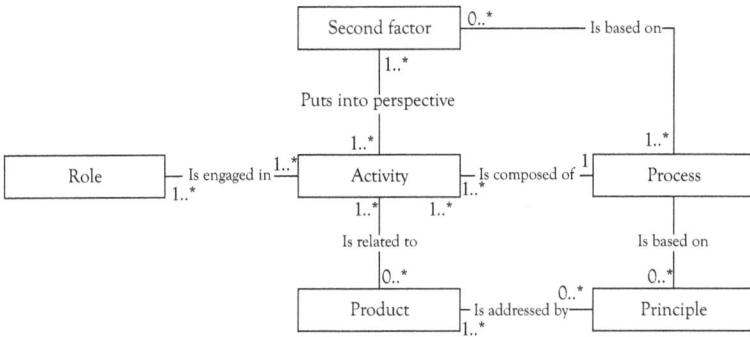

Figure 1.2 HybridP3M meta-model

core structure of the meta-model, including the second factor and, to a lesser extent, the independent aspect (indirect factor). Essentially, the process model consists of process descriptions, which can be captured as text, represented by figures, or embedded in web-based tools. The process model is basically the meta-model at work. It covers real examples, instances of specific meta-model elements. For example, a process description of planning may explain the relationship with specific roles engaged or define subprocesses as part of planning. On Insight Intranet, you can find examples of web-based process models, including PRINCE2 and ProwLO. Note that these two methodologies have a similar meta-model to HybridP3M (which should be the standard). The Praxis framework, on the other hand, has a different meta-model due to the fact of its larger scope (e.g., covering competence and capability maturity). But if you focus on the latter method in terms of process model, a weakness becomes apparent: it does not (yet) have well-defined roles or principles, admitted by the owner. In conclusion, HybridP3M's process model is shaped by its meta-model.

Process Aspects

HybridP3M's processes, which will be introduced in the following section, differentiate from competition from a closer analysis by process aspects. An analysis of processes based on process aspects helps to differentiate them among each other and to position them better (as compared to competing processes from other frameworks or from a higher point of view). It is meta-data about the processes. The five chosen conceivable process aspects are: (1) knowledge nature, (2) manageability, (3) specialization, (4) IT support, and (5) complexity. Maybe surprisingly, agility is not chosen. Agility is simply perceived as the outcome of a process or combination of processes. Obviously, process characteristics contribute to agility, but it is difficult to define a process in terms of agility due to the limited scope of processes (bound by process goals) and complex meaning of agile. By reading this guide, a better understanding of agile will gradually develop.

Knowledge nature is a tacit-explicit knowledge continuum. Processes that depend on explicit knowledge can be taught from books and other explicit sources, while processes that depend on tacit knowledge require personal experience to master them. Manageability refers to a step-by-step process versus skilled activity continuum. A step-by-step process can be easily followed and mastered by internalization, whereas a skilled activity requires practical experience and is not necessarily a linear sequence. A step-by-step process is manageable because it is easier to institutionalize with the help of explicit artifacts (like guides or web-based material). Also training material is easier to develop. Promoting skilled activity, on the other hand, requires other, more complex interventions such as learning on the job. Inspired by the distinction of management versus specialist products in PRINCE2, the third process aspect is specialization. But unlike PRINCE2's interpretation (where specialists have technical roles), even within the domain of management there are specializations. So project management is a management-specialist continuum. The fourth process aspect, IT support, is a scale of available IT support in the context of a process. Some processes more than others can benefit from the use of tools. Automation, with the advent of AI, has also become increasingly more realistic, at least in theory. Finally, complexity is a task complexity scale. Complexity depends on a multitude of activities, activity process flows, the number of roles and actors involved, and task difficulty. While an assessment of processes using scales and continuums is rather an arbitrary assignment open to debate, the assessments in this book are compensated by additional explanations.

HybridP3M's Processes

HybridP3M consists of the following processes, in any particular order:

- Defining the project or program
- Integrating knowledge management
- Planning
- Mitigating risks
- Business case development
- Realizing benefits
- Monitoring and control
- Managing stakeholder expectations
- Managing requirements
- Evaluating the project or program
- Leading the project or program
- Project/program establishment
- Providing assurance
- Agile product delivery.

For each process there is a devoted chapter. In these chapters, the processes are elaborated in great detail. This section only provides a basic understanding of each process.

Defining the Project or Program

Defining the project or program is the process that gives projects and programs existence and shape. Thanks to definition, projects and programs can be differentiated from business as usual and managed as unique undertakings. Definition covers written text, including various statements but also informal communication. In terms of content, definition also pays attention to the management environment that needs to be created to facilitate the technical challenges.

Integrating Knowledge Management

Integrating knowledge management is the process that merges the discipline of knowledge management with project processes. Knowledge management solves many problems at various levels. At the project level, for example, it helps to close knowledge and experience gaps. At the portfolio level, for example, it helps to close the gap between project-based learning and organizational learning, which implies that learning is shared beyond project boundaries and across teams. Knowledge management is a distinct process, supporting other project processes, including project management. Thanks to this kind of acknowledgment and one devoted process, HybridP3M is the only project and program methodology that respects knowledge management properly. While the Praxis framework addresses knowledge management, it provides very limited guidance. HybridP3M is closely aligned with the "Projects with Learning Outcomes" (ProwLO) methodology, through the third matrix (mapping between HybridP3M's and PRINCE2's processes), as will become apparent in the next chapter.

Planning

Planning is the process that anticipates (project or program) outcomes and defines a path to accomplish goals, taking into account constraints such as budget, time, and resources. Planning depends on the delivery model. In case of predictive or waterfall models, planning defines most project activity and, based on estimates, may provide realistic schedules. In such cases, project execution is usually governed by different levels of plans, including a project plan, stage plans, and optionally team plans (see PRINCE2). The project plan is first created at the beginning of a project, an upfront investment, and provides a baseline in the process of project evaluation. A predictive environment with a baseline plan enables management-by-exception, a PRINCE2 principle, characteristic of traditional project management. In case of Agile delivery methods, upfront planning is elusive due to the incremental and iterative nature of delivery. In such cases, a baseline project plan has little guiding and evaluation value. In turn, the live project plan (continuously updated based on progress) would become too dynamic and thus become a historical record of dynamic change instead of a container with predictive capability. So instead of using project plans, planning in the context of Agile delivery is mainly limited to prediction of small increments (also known as sprints in software development) and the equivalent concept of team plans (detailed plans at a very granular level). But irrespective of the delivery model, the Stage Gate paradigm must be enforced allowing management-by-stages, another PRINCE2 principle. This principle is essential for traditional project management and ProwLO's approach to project knowledge management (see Chapter 3). So HybridP3M must somehow combine the organization of projects and programs in stages with the planning of small increments. To the question of: is there a need for planning small increments at all? The answer is yes, for the coordination of teams.

Mitigating Risks

Mitigating risks is the process that identifies threats based on probability and impact resulting in risk (defined as potential damage due to vulnerability). It is also the process that, proactively, provides countermeasures to prevent risks from materializing, or preparations minimizing damage in the event risks materialize. When risks are residual, that is, cannot be prevented from occurring in the first place, only the second type of measure helps (anticipated reactive intervention). This process enables rational decision-making dealing with uncertainty. Thanks to risk identification, external and internal factors that can jeopardize project outcomes can be anticipated. However, in practice, there are always emergent factors that are unforeseen events. Emergent factors ultimately decide on risk and project behavior, limiting the effectiveness of risk management. While risk management is a useful tool, it should not become another mystique, a recipe for success (founded on manageability). From a traditional point of view, mitigating risks is partly dictated by risk tolerance. Depending on risk tolerances specific to certain risks, the priority of countermeasures can be established. Overall risk tolerance influences the business case as risks are an essential element of a business case. So the conclusion of business case viability and, thus, project or program beginning and continuation is partly shaped by risk tolerance.

Business Case Development

Business case development is the process that assesses project or program viability. A business case is a formal, dynamic document (as in, e.g., PRINCE2) that provides justification for carrying out projects or programs. It is a decision-making tool to start the project or program, or to stop it prematurely, saving costs. In other words, as a project unfolds, the business case provides justification for its continuation. Thus, it has to be revisited periodically or in a more ad hoc fashion as new data becomes available. There are many potential triggers for the evaluation of a business case, including changes in the environment, discovery of wrong assumptions, or the start of a new stage with additional planning data. The key element of the business case is the cost–benefits analysis.

Realizing Benefits

Realizing benefits is the process that links project or program goals with business strategy and takes advantage of arising opportunities as projects or programs unfold. Taking advantage means exploitation. Projects and programs are not stand-alone ventures; they are linked with permanent organizations with a long-term strategy. Realizing benefits transcends project processes and is rooted in portfolio management, which in turn is highly influenced by corporate management. This shows that the management of project and programs is a P3M or even corporate challenge (calling for cross-functional alignment), supporting the belief that project management and program management should evolve into a P3M-integrated discipline (first started with the Praxis framework). Realizing benefits motivates Agile behavior. As new opportunities may arise over the course of time, any project, program, or portfolio should have enough flexible capability to incorporate specific changes, to the benefit of the wider organization. Adjusting to these opportunities may alter project and program goals and consequently induce change in the delivery process. Alternatively, depending on the type of opportunity, portfolio management may trigger new projects and programs. Linking project or program goals with business strategy calls for alignment. While business strategy drives projects and programs (based on their anticipated added value), it may also evolve based on their actual outcome (by reflecting on their realized value). A well-defined, comprehensive P3M process of realizing benefits contributes to Agile performance. After project or program completion, when technical solutions are still in service (as part of the product's life cycle), realizing benefits may still trigger new increments for modification of the solution based on new opportunities (calling for new features) or a product improvement policy.

Monitoring and Control

Monitoring and control (M&C) is the process that ensures project or program goals are adhered to and correctly implemented based on the blueprint of planning. To this end the M&C process must maintain a stable management environment and prevent discrepancy between plans and actual progress. So project or program definition and planning provide the foundation for M&C. M&C is essentially a traditional process striving for predictive project behavior helped by accurate planning. M&C differs depending on the delivery model. In case of predictive or waterfall, M&C focuses on a successful execution of plans. Progress is managed based on a set of tolerances, corresponding to the principle of management-by-exception. In case of Agile delivery, M&C is reduced to people control as there are no comprehensive and detailed plans to guide progress. Without specified and agreed tolerances (due to a lack of baseline plans) management-by-exception is not an option. People control, a form of social control based on culture (foremost shared values) and molded by leadership (a distinct HybridP3M process), helps to establish predictive behavior aligned with project or program goals. But thanks to the Stage Gate paradigm, the project board, or other decision-making authority, any project or program has a controlled start, middle, and end (as also propagated by PRINCE2). By defining stages, decision moments can be planned to decide on the continuation of projects and programs, an essential form of control according to traditional philosophy that works with different delivery models (as reflected by, e.g., PRINCE2 Agile).

Managing Stakeholder Expectations

Managing stakeholder expectations is the process that informs stakeholders of progress in reality and, at the same time, tries to manipulate project behavior so that progress more closely follows stakeholder expectations. The latter can be achieved based on changing the conditions of the management environment (e.g., tweaking the process model or project organization) or various management interventions, centered on project acceleration (the time dimension), cost control (the cost dimension), quality improvement (the quality dimension), risk management (the risk dimension), or increasing benefits (the benefits dimension). Ultimately, stakeholders seek project success, a rather personal perception, which can be quantified based on objective measures. In Chapter 12, an attempt is made to rationalize project success (in the context of project and program evaluation). Basically, managing stakeholder expectations is to ensure the project or program is perceived as a success by all stakeholders, with a high rate of customer satisfaction—related to the overall process as well as end-result—as an important criterion. Adequate communication is an important prerequisite in the process.

Managing Requirements

Managing requirements is the process that uses feedback to develop required solutions, from project inception to handover moments, as far as in the maintenance phase, until product end of use (so the complete product life cycle), and that integrates requests for change with minimal delay and cost in the delivery process. Note that in software development, with the advent of DevOps, the transition from a project to business as usual, marked by the end of a project, is blurred as product development organized as a project (a traditional assumption) merges with operations and quality assurance. In a way, DevOps is the antithesis of conventional project and program management with a limiting life cycle and predetermined time band. HybridP3M's P3M approach, linking interdependent functions by exposing interfaces between them, may block the DevOps trend by providing a more traditional alternative. Management of requirements involves the translation of customer demand into a set of non-conflicting requirements that can provide the foundation for feasible solutions. In software development, it is common that when you combine elements the "solution" is limited due to inherent restrictions and design choices. So the capture of requirements automatically leads to the discovery of restrictions and possibly new requirements imposed by these restrictions. In other words, an intricate net of requirements will develop subject to rules and conventions inherent to technology. In practice, specifications lacking detail (high-level requirements) enable creativity and developer initiative, a trade-off with implications for risk. Generally, agility depends on a flexible adaptation of requirements (maintaining a feasible product that can be easily adjusted) and effective and efficient implementation of new features as required.

Evaluating the Project or Program

Evaluating the project or program is the process that reflects on project performance, answers to project success, and provides learning opportunities. Relatively speaking, it is not so popular in practice, despite its importance. This is related to the fact that learning organizations are not quite common. Empirical data shows that there are hardly, if any, optimized organizations with high maturity levels. Systematic learning, such as enabled by repeated evaluation, is typical for organizations with the highest level of maturity. Only systematic learning enables optimization, and both are still lacking in P3M environments. So is, generally speaking, a culture of learning, a precondition for learning. The role of knowledge management, increasingly recognized as a project success factor, plays a pivotal role in changing this situation. Evaluating the project or program is an ambiguous project management and knowledge management process. Since facilitating learning and increasing the learning capability of project members is a specialization, the project knowledge manager plays a critical role in this evaluation process. The project manager, on the other hand, should focus on the analysis of project performance using any available baselines: a clear role division.

Leading the Project or Program

Leading the project or program is the process that relates to the people side of management in P3M environments, building relationships and dividing labor at the same time. Leadership is all about leading processes, less about the people who are in charge, a rather unconventional proposition (but not novel). This proposition is founded on the belief that both leaders and followers are equally important in creating behavior serving common interests aligned with process goals or higher-level common goals (based on shared values). In other words, also followers are shaping processes. They are leaders in their own right. In the context of projects and programs, leadership means different things at different levels. At a high level, leadership is (general) conduct according to a project or program vision, facing uncertainty and risk common to P3M. For example, having the courage to deal with a technical challenge. At a lower level, leadership is managing teams in the context of product delivery (i.e., people management). Leadership is by no means an isolated process but relates to other HybridP3M processes by various acts. For example, selecting the right people for the project, as part of project establishment, is an act of leadership. Yet it is treated as a distinct process because it has great significance and impact on project behavior. Without leadership, management interventions are just decisions made on paper, not embodied by real people. Qualities like the ability to convince people of the necessity of certain actions are quite essential. Building on the earlier proposition, such qualities could be developed by both leaders and followers. If that is the case, leadership becomes dynamic with potentially shifting roles, in which followers take on the role of leader, and vice versa. This alternative approach to leadership not necessarily contradicts with clear lines of authority and undermines decision-making (very traditional principles). Process leadership, as to label this approach, may result in greater tolerance to changes (corresponding to an agile mindset) and foster a greater support base for decisions made (or yet to be made), primarily thanks to better understanding (indicating effective leadership).

Project/Program Establishment

Project/program establishment is the process that assigns people to roles based on responsibilities, reinforces any hierarchical lines of authority based on organizational design, and, through representation, creates an image of a group of people. Projects and programs are represented by their members and stakeholders. Altogether, they form the establishment. Members want to identify with successful projects as successful actors or teams (for the sake of career, status, etc.) and external opinion—based on image and exposure of project data—may lead to goodwill. So, practically, project establishment involves filling in leadership positions and clever resource management according to an organizational model, but also has a (cognitive) psychological dimension, with implications for leadership, public relations, and team building. From a management point of view, organizational design is a key subprocess as it provides an important foundation for the management environment, with implications for hierarchy and processes, calling for overall methodological alignment. The management environment is generally formed by people and culture (a key organizational dimension), protocols, conventions, and adopted models. Organizational design is followed by job assignments, that is to say, the allocation of people. Assigning people is a rational, match-making (capacity-related), or political (more random) process—in reality a spectrum, depending on leadership (i.e., the decision-makers), and type of position (management or technical). In conclusion, project/program establishment is a matter of organization but also representation.

Providing Assurance

Providing assurance is the process that aligns project processes to organizational standards and procedures based on monitoring and intervention. Intervention may imply enforcement of organizational standards. Providing assurance is highly influenced by the corporate quality assurance (QA) function, but it is not their responsibility. In the context of projects and programs, QA is limited to auditing (with similar process goals), a regular feature but not a repeated process. Instead, providing assurance is the responsibility of project board members (OGC 2009), people who decide on the viability of the project or program. The project board or equivalent groups of people are senior members with a great understanding of the value of corporate standards. So thanks to their continuous involvement in projects or program, the benefits of providing assurance can be guaranteed. The main benefit is arguably process consistency across projects. Depending on the application area, standards are co-developed, including the adoption and adaptation of standards derived from external sources, by quality analysts and the project management office. So the project board relies on their work.

Agile Product Delivery

Agile product delivery is the process that accelerates the development of technical solutions adjusted to dynamic changes in requirements, focused on the delivery of working parts, which can be evaluated, and just-in-time modified without compromising project or program objectives. This implies a close cooperation with customers for their essential input in the delivery process, calling for feedback processes. Accelerated development is achieved based on shorter rework cycles, thanks to a timely intervention by change authorities. Agile product delivery in HybridP3M is a structured process supported by formal change procedure, not unpredictable behavior with a disregard for earlier agreed project goals and objectives. Accordingly, this process is not conflicting with the traditional notion of a controlled environment. But Agile product delivery does limit upfront planning. Consequently, M&C is no longer guided by planning due to the lack of baselines (a traditional control mechanism). Traditionally, plans were used as a tool to predict and identify the exceeding of tolerances (at various levels depending on the level of plan), aligned with the principle of management-by-exception. In an Agile setting, tolerances are made independent from planning deliverables and adjusted to flexible stages with more uncertain length and cost. In practice, this means that exceptions are limited to project-level tolerances (i.e., overall budget, duration requirements). In other words, contractual agreement should take into account the limitations of detailed planning. Agile product delivery is also a mindset: to deliver value to customers as quick as possible. Improvement of the product based on additional increments, iterative or not, has become the new standard. Depending on the industry and project type, this kind of approach makes the delivery of a stable, final product within project or program boundaries (characterized by limited time and budget) more and more elusive. Agile product delivery, although very popularized, is not something radically new. Its significance is rooted in contradiction with a waterfall delivery model. HybridP3M acknowledges that the choice for a specific delivery model involves a trade-off between predictability and flexibility, as long as the industry permits, and favors in this respect Agile delivery.

CHAPTER 2

Method Foundation

In this chapter, a case is made for hybrid project management, which is a complex concept, often misinterpreted. Second, following the meta-model in the previous chapter, HybridP3M processes are linked with roles. This mapping is known as Matrix 1. The roles introduced here are explained in detail. Following this, Matrix 2 is introduced for matrix-style resource management, enabling optimized allocation of resources within a portfolio. Resource management in project-based organizations is per definition a P3M task. Next, Matrix 3 is introduced in which HybridP3M processes are mapped with PRINCE2 processes. The rationale behind Matrix 3 is to extend functional processes with life cycle management, characteristic for PRINCE2. After Matrix 3, building on the first section containing some definitions, arguments are provided to support the proposition that HybridP3M is both Agile and traditional. Next, HybridP3M principles are introduced, also based on the meta-model in the previous chapter. Finally, there is a section on knowledge-based project/program management, the adopted philosophy behind project management.

Building upon the meta-model, in the following process chapters, activities are addressed, the central element of process models in general and a key concept of the meta-model, providing the foundation for methodology development, and thus HybridP3M method definition. As activities relate to products or similar constructs, the latter are introduced as well. The process-data models in this book, introduced at the beginning of each process chapter, capture both elements. The HybridP3M processes are derived from the second factor, namely enterprise functions. For example, the HybridP3M process of risk management, or managing risk, is based on the function risk management. The HybridP3M processes are called functional for a reason. As a result, the entire meta-model is applied in this book.

A Case for Hybrid Project Management

A careful analysis of available project management methodologies in the public domain reveals that there is most certainly a need for another coherent approach. Those actors on the look for something new (post best practice era dominated by various process-based guides) nowadays concentrate on hybrid models combining Agile with traditional management associated with waterfall product delivery. The incentives to develop something new include process dissatisfaction and the fact that project failure still remains a major problem. The choice to combine Agile with more traditional approaches is probably the right one. The distinction between Agile and traditional has been challenged by some (e.g., Adrian Dooley on social media in 2020), suggesting it is a poor dichotomy and spectrum instead. Commenting on this calls the need for well-established definitions. The following definition of Agile is adopted:

> *"Agile methodology is a type of project management process where demands and solutions evolve through the collaborative effort of self-organizing and cross-functional teams and their customers."*
>
> —Muslihat, 2010

And the following new definition of traditional project management is proposed:

> Traditional methodology is the type of project management process where management control imposed by authority contributes to a controlled environment fostering predictability, and where changes are met with formal change management procedure.

According to the above definition, one can conclude that traditional project management does not equal a waterfall delivery model, which so many people believe. It is a matter of terminology calling for a paradigm shift. Similarly, while most Agile methods indicate an Agile delivery model, it is theoretically possible to apply Agile principles or other elements in waterfall or similar settings. As noted in the Introduction, agile or agility is a variable. Also, by comparing the two definitions, one can conclude that both concepts are not mutually exclusive. Considering the opposing philosophies, one can acknowledge that there is a dichotomy, but by combining both approaches into a new one, the result is indeed a methodology across the Agile–traditional spectrum. It should be noted that an alternative term for a waterfall delivery model is predictive.

Matrix 1: HybridP3M Processes and Roles

HybridP3M is characterized by decentralization of project management processes. Traditionally, it was the project manager who was responsible for the overall project management process, assisted by team managers (if applicable), project support staff, and supported by project board members. This traditional approach is arguably too demanding for one person. It is much better to delegate responsibility for some of the essential project processes to specialists, or at least make it a joint responsibility. In terms of hierarchy, the new project manager manages the project management team, reporting to the project board, while team managers or team leaders manage groups of technical specialists, being responsible for product delivery. So the project board, responsible for project direction, is excluding from the established project management team as proposed here, but nonetheless plays a key role in project processes. Matrix 1, divided in two parts, provides a mapping of HybridP3M's processes with specific roles engaged (see Tables 2.1 and 2.2). Following, each role is addressed in more detail. The processes are elaborated in following chapters.

Project Manager

The project manager is a people manager, generalist, and process champion. He or she is closely involved with 11 out of 14 of HybridP3M's processes. The only processes without a key involvement are managing requirements, providing assurance, and Agile product delivery. In case of the other processes, the project manager is often assisted by other roles, specialists. Project management skills are transferable, that is, they are effective in any industry and any type of project or program. The latter implies that technical expertise is advantageous but not crucial.

Table 2.1 *Mapping processes and roles*

	Project manager	Project knowledge manager	Project board members	Project support	Team manager	Corporate management
Defining the project/program	x		x	x		
Integrating knowledge management	x	x	x	x (training in tools)		
Planning	x	x (KM activities)				
Mitigating risks	x					
Business case development	x					
Realizing benefits	x		x			x
Monitoring and control	x		x			
Managing stakeholder expectations	x			x (handling communication; quantifying project success)		
Managing requirements						
Evaluating the project or program	x	x	x			x
Leading the project or program	x	x	x	x	x	x
Project establishment	x				x	x (resource management)
Providing assurance			x			
Agile product delivery		x (closing knowledge gaps)			x	

Table 2.2 *Mapping Processes and Roles*

	Business analyst	Financial specialist	Planner	Controller	Risk manager	Lead technical expert
Defining the project/program	x				x	
Integrating knowledge management						
Planning			x			x
Mitigating risks					x	
Business case development		x			x	
Realizing benefits		x				
Monitoring and control				x		
Managing stakeholders expectations						
Managing requirements	x					x
Evaluating the project or program						
Leading the project or program	x	x	x	x	x	x
Project establishment						
Providing assurance						
Agile product delivery	x		x	x		x

The potential technical knowledge and experience gaps of the project manager are, for example, compensated by knowledgeable team managers who are directly involved in the management of technical specialists. For example, in cases where there is no separate team manager—role fulfilled by one project manager—the project manager is supported by lead technical experts, the business analyst, and the project knowledge manager. The latter role identifies knowledge and experience gaps of the project manager in order to close them, for example, thanks to knowledge brokering. The project manager represents the project management team to the project board and is the head, a key player part of the project establishment.

Project Knowledge Manager

The project knowledge manager is someone who has a significant impact on knowledge processing, a knowledge management process champion, and operates based on a long-term knowledge management vision. This long-term focus extends the traditional project or program goals as how to get from State A to State B as quickly, cheaply, and effectively as possible (Barnes 2002). In the context of projects, he reports to the project manager. And in the context of a corporation, he reports to the senior knowledge management role in an organization, like head of knowledge or chief knowledge officer. This role is important for the project or program and the organization as a whole. The project knowledge manager, ideally armed with the Projects with Learning Outcomes (ProwLO) methodology, a companion method for HybridP3M, plays a role in solving or mitigating three key business problems: (1) reinventing the wheel, (2) repeating of mistakes, and (3) closing knowledge/experience gaps. These specific knowledge management problems relate to the project or program level but also have an organizational dimension to them. For example, reinventing the wheel depends on required knowledge and available knowledge organization-wide. Thus, it can be prevented if the required knowledge exists in the organization and is made available to the project.

Project Board Members

Project board members are responsible for project direction, the top-level subfunction of projects (above project management). Project directing results in a process by the same name. HybridP3M decided not to incorporate this process as a distinct, main process. Instead, directing a project is a subprocess of project or program leadership as performed by the project board. In addition, the project board is involved in other HybridP3M processes. The project board is represented by the main stakeholders of project or program, key decision-makers responsible for project initiation, and has the authority to prematurely end the project. Typically, the project board comprises the business case owners in a commercial customer–supplier environment, the customer, and senior supplier. Following PRINCE2, another project board role is the senior user, representing the people who will be using the end-product. In the process of handover, the customer has to accept the results, and in the wider process of closing the project, the project board in general has to agree on project closure.

Project Support

The project support function is an ad hoc service originating from the project management office, a line function complementing temporary project or program structures. Project management offices are a complex concept with many potential subfunctions, depending on scope and organizational maturity. They deserve a guide on their own. But in the context of HybridP3M's processes, it suffices to understand their role in relation to a few processes. Project support, mainly administrative support and limited specialist support (specialists are likely different roles), plays a part in the preparation of project documentation. This provides an opportunity to be directly involved with the contents of various definition deliverables. Thus, project support helps to define the project and program, capitalizing on previous projects. At the same time, it ensures that documents have a style (format and writing) consistent to corporate standards. Project support also plays a part in integrating knowledge management, specifically providing training in the use of knowledge management systems. Finally, project support plays a role in managing stakeholder expectations based on accumulated communication expertise, advising the project manager or even performing communication tasks, and quantifying project success based on objective measures, which may prevent contractual disagreements.

Team Manager

The team manager is the role that primarily oversees and leads Agile product delivery. This role may influence project establishment by proposing team members based on individual networks. Ultimately, however, the project manager and corporate management responsible for resource management decide on allocating people. It is essential that the team manager has an agile mindset and it is highly recommended that he or she had agile training on various Agile approaches. After all, the more knowledge and experience, the better in the light of knowledge-based project management. On the other hand, Agile product delivery in HybridP3M is not a submethodology, as compared to PRINCE2-Agile, relating the PRINCE2 methodology to Agile methods like, for example, Scrum as an overarching framework. So, while process awareness is key, the team manager is not necessarily a process champion, but rather a people manager.

Corporate Management

The involvement of corporate management depends on the management environment, whether it is a commercial supplier environment or a project or program executed in-house. In case of the former, corporate managers associated with each business case owner play a role in leading the project or program, aligning their business case with corporate goals. So, in practice, if there are multiple business cases, the corporate management of the different organizations takes responsibility for the different business cases involved, showing commitment and leadership where necessary. A party that is responsible for both project management and delivery also deals with resource management, allocation of people based on specific project roles, and thus plays a key role in project establishment. Portfolio management could be considered an aspect of corporate management if not established as a specialist function within an organization.

Business Analyst

The business analyst plays a key role in establishing requirements, and thereby the scope of the solution to be developed. He or she translates customer demand into a set of requirements that can be implemented, provided that specific requirements are feasible. Customer demand relates to not only technical aspects but also the management environment. The customer may have his own approach to project or program management, based on corporate standards. This approach, translated into another set of requirements (management-related), is *not* the concern of the business analyst. The design of the management environment—part of defining a project or program—is solely the responsibility of the project manager, in cooperation with the customer, bearing in mind that project processes must be aligned with HybridP3M. So the business analyst limits himself to the technical side of the project. In terms of project or program definition, he or she contributes to the definition of the solution to be developed and also the method or method(ology) of delivering that solution as long as the latter does not conflict with the management approach established by the project manager. In terms of leadership, the business analyst must be proactive and safeguard Agile product delivery, closely cooperating with the team managers.

Financial Specialist

The financial specialist is responsible for business case development and realizing benefits, together with other involved roles. With his or her financial expertise, the financial specialist judges the business case from a financial perspective. Every business case owner in a project or program should have his own financial specialist. If project management is outsourced to the main supplier, then the financial specialist of the supplier organization is also responsible for the customer business case. Financial reward, that is, return on investment, is one of the most important benefits of projects and programs that needs to be managed. This type of management involves financial analysis, taking into account project or program budget. Disregarding potential conflicting financial interests, it is key to ensure on-budget delivery as on-budget delivery is a measure for project success. Projects and programs have business outcomes; getting paid for work is just one aspect driving supplier business operations. The financial analyst should define these business outcomes together with the project manager and project board in order to be able to estimate the total value that can be attributed to specific undertakings.

Planner

The planner role depends on the delivery model. In case of predictive/waterfall delivery, the planner creates and maintains project planning, which provides the basis for monitoring and control. Well-defined activity and accurate estimates are essential in such kind of environment. In case of an Agile delivery model, the planner is mainly occupied with planning iterative increments in the context of stages. Flexible stages merely provide the context, and thus, with limited upfront planning, stage plans no longer serve monitoring and control purposes. They are simply a function of team plans covering increments, not guiding material. Similarly, the project plan has no predictive capability as projects are too dynamic and continuously subject to change. Rather, the planning of increments drives a history of project planning, the "Project History Plan." The usefulness of a project plan in such agile environment is restricted. In case of Agile delivery, one of the main reasons to create a project plan is the process to make ball park estimates, meaningful to budgeting.

Controller

The controller role just like the planner role depends of the delivery model. In case of predictive/waterfall delivery, the controller is responsible for monitoring and controlling based on project planning baselines. If one or more project tolerances are expected to be exceeded, the controller has to define corrective measures in discussion with the project manager and implement them in agreement with the project manager, who may escalate the issue to the project board depending on his or her expert judgment of the necessity to do so. Escalating issues to the project board is mandatory if despite the planned corrective measure the tolerances are expected to be exceeded. In case of Agile product delivery, monitoring and control is performed without project planning baselines. Additionally, the controller should assure that product delivery is indeed agile, according to well-defined and established agility criteria. Furthermore, the controller ensures that project processes do not compromise project goals. In some cases, monitoring and control may lead to change in project assumptions due to feedback from live processes. In other words, the controller plays a pivotal role in making sure that project goals are realistic. The latter responsibility calls for a close cooperation with the project manager, responsible for the business case.

Risk Manager

The risk manager is a well-established specialist role in the field of project management. In many industries and organizations, project managers are supported by risk managers. This trend supports the foundation of a matrix organization. Risks affect the business case and thus are part of business case development. Risk definition is part of project and program definition in general.

Lead Technical Experts

Also, technical specialists matter in the context of project and program management. They are represented by one or more lead technical experts. Rather than just following instructions on what to do, they jointly shape (with planners) the flow of activity and estimate duration (usually in man-hours). Together with the business analyst, they manage requirements by translating them into work. Also they help define requirements, or at least externalize, that were not captured from the customer. They are "leading" the technical delivery, and thus have a great impact on project processes. Their formal leaders are team managers, leading product delivery from a management perspective.

Matrix 2: Matrix-Style Resource Management

Matrix 1 on process–role relations dictates that project and program management is delegated to specialists; it is a joint effort. Matrix 2, used for assigning people having specific roles to projects, additionally assumes that one person can have multiple roles. This applies to single projects as well as to a portfolio. For example, a project manager can be also a business analyst and/or team manager. Table 2.3 indicates how assignment of people can be put into practice. The processes in this table correspond to HybridP3M processes. People allocation is part of resource management

Table 2.3 Example of Matrix 2

	Person A: Role 1	Person A: Role 2	Person B: Role 1	Person C: Role 3	Etc.
Project 1	Process X, Process Y	Process Z		Process T	
Project 2			Process X, Process Y	Process T	
Etc.					

in the context of portfolio management. Efficient use of Matrix 2 calls for software aid, such as spreadsheet software.

Table 2.3 Example of Matrix 2

Matrix 3: Extending HybridP3M Processes with PRINCE2's Life Cycle Management

A key strength of PRINCE2 is how it identifies various stages of a project life cycle. Following PRINCE2's process model, the life cycle dictates project processes. But PRINCE2 is mistaken by the prescriptive quality of its key processes in terms of activities. So, at the process level, there are indeed distinguishable processes, but at the activity level, as a project unfolds, projects are not characterized by a uniform process. So the detailed process model of PRINCE2, its key characteristic, is also the weakness of PRINCE2. HybridP3M's processes better reflect actual project behavior, as it should be (to-be). So the best solution is to place HybridP3M's processes into perspective of life cycle management. In other words, to map HybridP3M processes with high-level PRINCE2 processes. However, it should be stressed that in practice, while useful, this mapping has limited prescriptive power. The reality of project behavior is much more complex and divergent. Exceptions in terms of processes are commonplace, and thus process models have limited generic validity (i.e., applicability in different situations).

The development of Matrix 3: HybridP3M–PRINCE2 Mapping consists of two steps. The goal is to adopt a custom-made matrix given organizational focus and organizational life cycle management. The first step is to identify the relevance of a HybridP3M process in the context of a PRINCE2 process (link HybridP3M to life cycle management), which implies putting a cross in table indicating relevance (essentially a vague reference). Based on this initial mapping, the second step is to be more specific and explain how a specific HybridP3M process takes shape in the context of life cycle management. The latter is essentially a matter of annotation for more specific guidance. Note that adopting Matrix 3 is an act of life cycle management and a part of project or program definition. Table 2.4 illustrates step 1, while Table 2.5 illustrates step 2. One conclusion that can be drawn from Table 2.4 is that specific HybridP3M processes are quite continuous, not isolated to specific life cycle processes.

What Makes HybridP3M Agile and Traditional at the Same Time?

HybridP3M is characterized by team dynamics in the project management team, a matrix organization, complemented with the project board, with often joint responsibility for processes. Teams are more adaptable to change as compared to single actors with personal bias. Coordination, alignment, team work, and multilateral communication all play a part in team dynamics. The leader paradigm, a single champion, is no longer sufficient to deal with complex and dynamic situations. Only groups of people with their own unique skillsets are able to cope with the complex demands as requested by projects and programs. The knowledge-intensive aspect of most projects and programs necessitates specialization in management as well as technical work. Specialization acknowledged and established in HybridP3M is the only possible answer to agility demands, such as adaptability in a group effort.

Second, HybridP3M is an advocate of Agile product delivery, a designated process with management implications, and which is supported by effective and continuous requirements management. Agile product delivery implies that delivery must be agile, a process outcome, as simple as that. The challenge here is to model a distinct agile process that differentiates from existing methods. The alternative is to adopt existing Agile methods (i.e., Agile delivery processes), like Scrum-based approaches. This happened with PRINCE2-Agile. But these existing methods are either not applicable across industry (usually focus on software development) or fabricate redundant roles and responsibilities, such as for example Scrum Masters.

Table 2.4 *Matrix 3 Based on Cross-references*

	Starting up a project	Initiating a project	Directing a project	Managing stage boundaries	Controlling a stage	Managing product delivery	Closing a project
Defining the project or program	x	x		x			
Integrating knowledge management	x	x	x	x	x	x	x
Planning	x	x		x	x	x	
Mitigating risks	x	x			x		
Business case development	x	x		x			
Realizing benefits	x	x	x				x
Monitoring and control			x	x	x	x	x
Managing stakeholder expectations	x	x	x	x	x	x	x
Managing requirements	x	x	x	x	x	x	x
Evaluating the project or program				x	x		x
Leading the project or program	x	x	x	x	x	x	x
Project/program establishment	x	x		x			
Providing assurance			x				
Agile product delivery				x		x	

Table 2.5 *Example of Matrix 3 with Annotations*

	Starting up a project	Initiating a project	Directing a project	Managing stage boundaries	Controlling a stage	Managing product delivery	Closing a project
Defining the project or program	Conceptualization of the project/program	Formal documentation of project/program entity		Project/program definition subject to dynamic business case, updated during stage transitions			
Integrating knowledge management	In staging an appropriate management environment, prior to project start, various management knowledge needs need to be satisfied	—Knowledge management practices need to be formally embedded in acknowledged project processes. —Adoption of the ProwLO methodology for project knowledge management	—Approval of project knowledge management processes. —Knowledge brokering. —Evaluation of knowledge needs satisfaction.	—Stage transitions provide an opportunity for evaluation, reflection, and learning.	—Live capture of knowledge demands knowledge management practice during a stage while executed. —Increasing the learning capability of project members thanks to knowledge management	Reuse of specialist, technical knowledge requires a knowledge management approach.	Knowledge management is relevant to project/program evaluation at the end.

(Continued)

Table 2.5 (*Continued*)

	Starting up a project	Initiating a project	Directing a project	Managing stage boundaries	Controlling a stage	Managing product delivery	Closing a project
Planning	Initial project/program vision, supported by feasibility, provides a starting point for allocation of time and resources, that is, the foundation of planning.	Project/program definition enables ball park estimates for an overall project plan, characterized by milestones.		—Stage transitions provide an opportunity to anticipate stage increments by gathering information on customer demand, and more specifically, high-priority requirements.	—Executed stages with live information need 'project history plans', not baseline files useful to project evaluation, enabling better coordination of subsequent stages and increments.	Planning increments should take into account agility (the ability to deal with change effectively and efficiently) and the effectiveness and efficiency of the production process, calling for coordination and task understanding.	
Mitigating risks	The success of project/program depends on risks and their management. Threats are inevitable in complex situations and should be identified upfront, from the very beginning of the project/program idea,	Based on new information about the management environment, the project approach, business case, etc., the risk management process can be formally embedded and become part of project/program culture.			Risk management is a continuous process, from project/program start, with direct impact on the current stage. The organization of projects/programs into stages is of less importance.		

| Business case development | —Anticipated benefits drive the vision behind a project/program. They form the foundation for a business case. | —Anticipated benefits are analyzed more thoroughly in order to prevent wishful thinking, and elaborated. —Quantifiable benefits that can be measured indicate a mature business case development process. | | —Stage transitions provide an opportunity to reflect on and update the business case. | |

(Continued)

Table 2.5 (*Continued*)

	Starting up a project	Initiating a project	Directing a project	Managing stage boundaries	Controlling a stage	Managing product delivery	Closing a project
Realizing benefits	—Business drives people to define and execute added value activity. Projects and programs are undertakings that unite activity toward common goals with promise of significant benefits to the organization. So people like to engage in projects/ programs, starting up a creative process prior to commitment of time and resources.	—In order to ensure commitment by senior members in an organization, for approval and support, the personal beliefs on commercial viability need to be founded on solid assumptions. During this process, these assumptions are defined and elaborated, so that they can be questioned.	—Senior management, including the project board, is concerned with the outcomes of a project/ program. So the whole process of project direction is directed toward achieving objectives in line with anticipated outcomes.				Some benefits can only be realized after a project/ program formally has ended. There should be a process planned in the future to revisit anticipated benefits and explore new opportunities related to a closing project. The definition and planning of this process should take place in closing a project.

Monitoring and control	—The project board monitors and controls the project/program based on the principles of management by exception, adjusted to delivery model, and management by stages. Anticipated project outcomes and set tolerances act as guidance.	The project manager applies the principle of management by stages, defined by key decision moments.	The project manager must prevent any form of escalation in the context of stages, either based on agreed tolerances or the complex notion of success. This means that issues must remain under control.	Product delivery must be monitored and controlled. Product delivery management (mainly performed by team managers) deals with this process, taking into account various requirements, including planning, functional and quality requirements.	A controlled end of a project/program demands some level of monitoring and control. This type of monitoring and control mainly takes place in the context of project evaluation and handover.

(Continued)

Table 2.5 (Continued)

	Starting up a project	Initiating a project	Directing a project	Managing stage boundaries	Controlling a stage	Managing product delivery	Closing a project
Managing stakeholder expectations	—Identification of all stakeholders, parties with a potential or actual interest in the project or program. Stakeholder analysis, which entails closer examination of interests, mutual interests, and potential use of incentives to combine interests.	—Taking into account stakeholders, definition of a communication strategy.	—The project board, representing key stakeholders, should be sensitive to other stakeholder's needs, on the board itself and beyond. This sensitivity should translate into communication tactics, aligned with the communication strategy. Communication tactics, in turn, drive communication, which should be timely, accurate, and goal-effective.	Stages mark transition moments, times for reflection, and communication. Key stakeholders should be updated on progress.	During the execution of a stage, the project manager can utilize highlight reports to keep project board members informed on the progress. The communication authorities for other stakeholders can use this report as input for their own communication efforts.	Stakeholders are interested in successful execution of product delivery, not necessarily every technical detail. They also must be reassured that the developed products or services comply to quality criteria.	Handover and delivery are moments to celebrate potential success. This requires sensitivity to ceremonial convention, impacting communication style.

Managing requirements	—Define customer demand according to an initial set of requirements. —Develop the initial requirements into a project approach of the solution to be developed.	—Update the requirements based on new information. —Consolidate the project approach; extend the project approach with the method(ology) on how to develop the anticipated solution, and thereby establish conditions and additional constraints.	—The project board as a whole must be informed about requirements management, including the process aspect, liaising with the business analyst.	—Stage transitions provide an opportunity to gather requirements for the next increments within a stage, which can be used for planning purposes.	Agile delivery demands continuous requirements management while a stage is executed.	Agile product delivery deals with ad hoc gathering of new requirements that emerge during the execution of work packages.	Reflecting on requirements management partly explains customer satisfaction with the output, the delivered solutions.
Evaluating the project or program				—The stage gate paradigm provides time and resources to execute evaluation during stage transitions.	Continuous live capture of knowledge, dictated by ProwLO, enables ad hoc reflection, on time.	How to make processes more effective next time in the context of a portfolio (e.g., how to improve project planning based on learning from project evaluation). How to ensure project success.	

(Continued)

Table 2.5 (Continued)

	Starting up a project	Initiating a project	Directing a project	Managing stage boundaries	Controlling a stage	Managing product delivery	Closing a project
Leading the project or program	—Leadership supporting process of goals of SU, including to establish a viable business case.	—Leadership supporting process goals of IP, including the establishment of a sound management environment.	—Leadership supporting process goals of DP, including stakeholder management, project assurance, and alignment with project goals.	—Leadership supporting process goals of SB, including sound decision making in the context of go-no-go decisions for the next planned stage.	Leadership supporting process goals of CS, including the capability to establish management by exception.	Leadership supporting process goals of MP, including agility in product delivery.	Leadership supporting process goals of CP, including a controlled end, and reflection on outcomes and project/program success.
Project/ program establishment	—Formation of the project board and project management team	—Formation of the project board and project management team —Establishment of lead technical specialists		—Allocation of additional project members depending on technical requirements			

Providing assurance		—The project board is solely responsible for providing assurance, in particular, alignment with corporate standards.		
Agile product delivery		—The stage gate paradigm provides control to the benefit of Agile product delivery. Organizing parallel technical phases in stages makes it possible to accelerate the project/program, but processes become more complex, less effective to exception management, and arguably less agile due to greater interdependencies.		Managing product delivery must become an agile process, requirements-driven, with flexible work packages.

HybridP3M also believes that the various notions introduced in Agile methods can be omitted and that Agile delivery should be extreme always, just like the Agile approach in software development of extreme programming (XP). This extreme approach should be combined with a work package management process, typical to PRINCE2, for greater control. This combination represents an agile alternative to Agile's interpretation of management control (popular Agile approaches). As a result, HybridP3M resembles PRINCE2-Agile but is more radical, eliminating the need to combine with existing Agile methods. Ultimately, the defined project approach decides on the type of solution and/or method of delivering that solution. So basically HybridP3M has adopted a process model that combines PRINCE2 with XP basics, but more generalized across industry (mainly for system engineering in general).

Agile *project* management, as opposed to mere delivery, is arguably a myth—it can be agile only to a certain extent. One means to make project management more agile is flexible processes with optional activities, lessening management overhead. Generally, project management has always been traditional and will remain that way. The foundations of the traditional school, originating from management literature, are difficult to question with. The key is to blend traditional project management and to adjust it with Agile product delivery. Depending on the delivery model, either predictive or Agile, there exist only *implications* for management, captured by the definition of the management environment. Predictive delivery is by nature less agile. Management is a control discipline, which makes sense as resources and knowledge are scarce or unevenly distributed. Therefore, traditional management is critical to make the right investments or to abandon ship when things go wrong. Similarly, premature ending of a project, a traditional notion, is not necessarily a bad thing and minimizes sunk costs (costs that no longer can be recovered). The challenge is to develop an integrated P3M solution, and HybridP3M answers this call thanks to an enterprise architecture orientation, also known as function orientation.

Given the fact that project and program organizations must be adaptable and flexible to change, traditional management must take into account agility. Essentially, traditional management remains the same process of control. Fortunately, well-established traditional project management methods have cleared the path for practitioners. However, they all failed to properly understand the Agile context. Either they neglect Agile or combine the two somewhat artificially like PRINCE2-Agile. Fundamentally speaking, a methodology should incorporate both Agile as well as traditional principles. HybridP3M's principles, reflecting this type of blending, are introduced in the next section.

Principles

HybridP3M comprises 11 unique and non-obvious principles and three obvious—common-sense—principles adopted from PRINCE2. The principles are grouped in categories for a better overview. The categories are management intervention, knowledge management and organizational learning, project characteristics, and corporate ambition. Management interventions include: (1) management by stages, (2) management by exception depending on the delivery model, and (3) effective change management procedure. Knowledge management and organizational learning include: (4) learning from experience, (5) integrated knowledge management, (6) increasing learning capability, and (7) personal knowledge mastery. Project characteristics include (8) continued business justification, (9) defined roles and responsibilities, (10) stable, non-ambiguous management environment, and (11) extensive project approach based on selected delivery model. And, finally, corporate ambition includes: (12) applied process, function, and knowledge orientation, (13) mature enterprise functions, and (14) agile mindset complementing a culture of management control.

The obvious principles adopted from PRINCE2 include:

- Continued business justification
- Learn from experience
- Defined roles and Responsibilities

Management by Stages

Management by stages is a principle adopted from PRINCE2. It is a traditional principle- based on the stage gate paradigm of projects and programs. The benefit of this principle is that projects and programs can be managed according to a life cycle approach, with controlled start, middle, and end. Stages are defined by key decision moments, and armed with the dynamic business case, the viability of projects and programs can be evaluated based on predefined time bands. Every new stage leads to go-no-go decisions, a perfect control mechanism.

Management by Exception Depending on the Delivery Model

Management by exception is based on the assumption that the management should intervene in projects and programs only in case the original planning is anticipated to be disrupted. Various tolerances determine if intervention is required. This approach frees the project management team and project board from constant involvement in daily project and program processes. However, it only works well in case of a predictive delivery model where planning provides useful baselines, and thus effective agreed tolerances. In case of Agile delivery, the management by exception principle is compromised. But generally, it holds that exceptions impacting project and program outcomes should be managed anyway in terms of issue management, with or without extensive planning. This has to do with the diverse nature of exceptions and the variety of potential issues as emergent factors. In other words, not every exception is rooted in planning. The ad hoc nature of management by exception is open to debate. Leadership processes may demand more active involvement of managers, especially in uncertain environments. Tacit knowledge will shape the practical implications of this principle, and thus scaling cannot be neglected.

Effective Change Management Procedure

Effective change management procedure is an essential management overhead required to handle change. Agile responsiveness to change needs to be complemented with formal change procedure for a controlled environment. To this end, the PRINCE2 2009 change control procedure is adopted, a modified version of the OGC (2005) change control technique. Issues such as off-specifications, requests for change, and problems/concerns are properly analyzed by this procedure. See OGC (2009), page 95, for more information.

Learning from Experience

Learning from projects and programs is a natural outcome. In practice, however, a knowledge management problem is that learning is not shared beyond teams, across the organization. To learn from experience is common sense, but in practice, learning is limited due to poorly executed project evaluation and limited learning capability of project members. As pointed out by John Dewey, "we do not learn from experience ... we learn from reflecting on experience" (Anirban Chatterjee on LinkedIn timeline 2020). So while this principle is common sense, in practice there are problems with learning. The principle of integrated knowledge management facilitates learning from experience.

Integrated Knowledge Management

In today's knowledge economy, the majority of projects and programs are knowledge-intensive. This characteristic combined with problems in organizational knowledge management calls for a knowledge management approach as part of the overall project approach. Thanks to the definition of the ProwLO methodology, knowledge management in project and program environments has become a feasible practice, optimizing knowledge processes within projects and programs and beyond.

Increasing Learning Capability

Learning capability relates to the proficiency of gaining new knowledge from experience. This requires additional reflection, dialogue, and discussion. Only with a knowledge management framework can additional dedication of time and resources be rationalized. Because thanks to adopting a formal knowledge management approach, learning becomes part of the project and program goals.

Personal Knowledge Mastery

Project members should be aware of the power of personal knowledge mastery. With organizational and project and program processes for knowledge management, effective knowledge application comes down to individual actors engaged in management and specialist processes. So there are multiple levels of knowledge management: organizational level, project or program level, group or team level, and, finally, individual level. Personal knowledge mastery deals with the individual level. Project members need to be familiar with the essence of knowledge, the diversity of various knowledge types, and how knowledge types relate to the exploitation of knowledge and creativity. Furthermore, by understanding the life cycle of knowledge, they can better relate to the process implications of project knowledge management. For example, when project members gain new experience and thus new knowledge, they, for example, will understand that the organizational value of their knowledge will increase if shared across the organization, or that the applicability in other contexts (i.e., other projects or programs) will increase if the knowledge is refined, resulting in generalization in the context of knowledge evaluation.

Continued Business Justification

It is common sense to only start viable projects and programs, depending on a business case. It is also common sense to prematurely end a project or program when costs outweigh claimed benefits. The business case is dynamic and subject to internal and external factors affecting viability.

Defined Roles and Responsibilities

Division of labor demands defined roles and responsibilities. It is common sense to sign contracts or acknowledge social contracts related to project and program work. In HybridP3M, the matrix organization provides a mechanism to establish roles and responsibilities, while the project establishment allocates people taking on certain roles and responsibilities. In PRINCE2, the product of job descriptions is used for project establishment. In HybridP3M, in contrast, project members have organizational specializations and sign social contracts per process basis, which is less bureaucratic.

Stable, Non-ambiguous Management Environment

The management environment is the total of social convention, common language, and formal procedure across project and program processes.

Explicit project documentation, including contracts, reinforces the management environment. The management environment must be stable and non-ambiguous in order to prevent different interpretations of processes and to ensure process consistency. More mature organizations have clearly defined corporate standards that make it easier to adopt a proven management environment. Common understanding of process requirements is a key success factor.

Extensive Project Approach Based on Selected Delivery Model

The project approach is a complex management product that shapes project and program processes. It should at least acknowledge consensus on Agile product delivery, specify the delivery model, describe the solution to be developed, and define or provide a reference to the adopted management methodology, like HybridP3M. The project approach provides a foundation for social contracts.

Applied Process, Function, and Knowledge Orientation

HybridP3M advocates a combination of process, function, and knowledge orientation. A process orientation on its own, the current status quo, is not enough to guarantee project and program success. An enterprise architecture orientation optimizes information flows between all enterprise functions relevant in the context of projects and programs. It is a tool for As-is and To-be analysis, revealing the intricate complexities of enterprise project and program management and depicting the P3M landscape as the context of projects and programs. But even a function orientation complementing process orientation has limitations, in particular with regard to knowledge management, which is essential for project excellence. Only an additional knowledge orientation provides the means to institutionalize optimization of processes. Optimization of processes requires state-of-the-art knowledge management in order to solve key KM problems. Systematic learning, characteristic of optimized organizations, can only be realized with sound knowledge management practices.

Mature Enterprise Functions

High organizational maturity leads to more proficient project and program processes based on the premise of optimization. Maturity development should thus be part of the mission, vision, and strategy of project-dependent and project-driven organizations. Maturity is a multidimensional concept consisting of five aspects: (1) strategy and policy, (2) organization and process, (3) monitoring and control, (4) people and culture, and (5) IT (adopted from Scheper 2002). This implies that adopting processes, thanks to the definition of a project approach, on its own is not enough. Other aspects should be taken care of as well; a holistic approach to maturity development is key.

Agile Mindset Complementing a Culture of Management Control

While a popular concept, Agile is prone to different interpretations. Although successful in software development, cross-industry applicability is not yet proven (in Turner, Maylor and Lee-Kelly 2014). This could be caused by the lack of cross-industry approaches. Also, Agile approaches are not holistic, with limited reference to project management best practices. Accordingly, Agile risks to be a management fad in the long term. To prevent this it is important to acknowledge the dynamic nature of projects and programs, the uncertainty element of change, and the impact of emergent factors, which never can be fully prevented. Awareness of such environments and contexts of projects and programs will lead to a realization that agility, defined as responsiveness to change and effective change management, cannot be neglected. The next step is to make project and program processes more flexible and adjusted to inevitable change, incorporating Agile in a traditional project/program management methodology. In any case, an agile mindset is required. Only with an agile mindset, project members will acknowledge the value of Agile processes in the context of a stable management environment, supported by a culture of management control. A culture of management control is a characteristic of mature enterprises. It is enabled by a well-defined project approach, institutionalized by the adoption of corporate standards and reinforced by project and program assurance.

Knowledge-Based Project/Program Management

Knowledge-based orientation is a characteristic of organizations with the highest possible level of organizational maturity, generally accepted as level 5 across different maturity models. It is an evolution from process-oriented project management followed by function-oriented project management. All three paradigms add up. So knowledge-based orientation also includes process orientation and function orientation. Figure 2.1 presents how these paradigms add up in more detail. The diagram is explained below. HybridP3M is associated with level 5, the optimal situation, but in practice, level 5 demands highest maturity levels across the dimensions of an organization: (1) strategy and policy, (2) organization and process, (3) monitoring and control, (4) people and culture, and (5) IT. So adopting HybridP3M is just one step of organizational development and requires investment in other areas.

Level 0 is characterized by random activity and lack of paradigmatic orientation. There is very limited understanding of what comprises effective project management, in all its complexity. Management of undertakings is based on a personal approach to management. The best example of level 0 are the projects in the *UK Apprentice* show, where one team member assumes the role of a project manager. In this show projects are characterized by defined objectives, and the project manager divides roles on sub teams. The projects are in fact mini-undertakings with limited complexity, thanks to clear objectives, a small time span, and clear task division.

Level 1 corresponds to an initial process. There are signs of process awareness, partly thanks to market-available best practice frameworks. Organizations at level 1 typically hire project management staff based on qualification, including specific certification. This is a form of people control. In practice, this approach leads to process diversity, depending on the knowledge and skills of project management staff. A single, uniform corporate approach is lacking. So there is nothing to adhere to, fueling ad hoc processes. In order to start developing and promoting corporate standards, the organization needs to mature further.

Level 2, corresponding to a repeated process, is a game changer. There is a basic process orientation, which means that project performance can be rationalized, looking for weak spots in terms of specific

Level 5	Optimized Process	Knowledge Orientation	Professionally managed knowledge advancing creative capability
Level 4	Managed Process	Function Orientation	Enterprise Architecture of interdependent functions with interfaces and information flows
Level 3	Defined Process	Advanced Process Orientation	Mature processes
Level 2	Repeated Process	Basic Process Orientation	Immature processes
Level 1	Initial Process	Qualification orientation	People control
Level 0	Random activity	No paradigmatic orientation	Personal approach to management

Figure 2.1 Levels of maturity and related concepts

processes. Typically, processes are analyzed by the project management office (PMO), which is responsible for the development of corporate standards. Based on their work and increasing process awareness by project members, project processes can be repeated across projects, but it is not necessarily the norm and relies of individual attitude and competence. Processes are generally immature, meaning not optimized. The effectiveness of managing identified processes is limited. Process improvement is neither structural nor coordinated, despite any possible good intentions of the PMO. The latter is caused by a lack of project assurance and poor functional interfaces (communication with the PMO).

Level 3, corresponding to a defined process, is characterized by an advanced process orientation. Processes are well defined and captured in corporate standards. The definition of processes is taken care of by a specialist process manager, assigned by the PMO. Processes are also monitored by the PMO, and enforced, thanks to project assurance, by the project board. The promotion of corporate standards is recognized as a key responsibility by the PMO who takes this responsibility seriously. The input for process improvement, however, is limited due to a lack of feedback processes from actual projects and programs. So process improvement is not yet structural.

Level 4 marks a shift toward function orientation. Thanks to a better understanding of enterprise functions and their interfaces, an advanced enterprise architecture emerges. Information flows between organizational functions provide valuable inputs for the optimization of processes. Without adequate information flows, an organization can never be fully aligned internally and externally. Based on an enterprise perspective driven by functional goals, processes can be managed and improved according to new insights and requirements. Level 4 is not an ideal situation, however, as there is limited integration of experiences in project processes, and the major pitfall is that the enterprise architecture becomes a static blueprint not adaptable to change. It is recommended to delegate enterprise architecture to a specialist enterprise architect.

Level 5, corresponding to an optimized process, is characterized by knowledge orientation, that is to say, knowledge-based project and program management. At level 5, organizations are learning continuously to improve conditions and processes. One condition for a successful learning organization is a culture of learning. Another condition is effective knowledge management processes, which are essential to integrate experience into project processes. Optimized process implies a balance between exploration and exploitation. Exploration is like learning, while exploitation builds on corporate standards in the form of blueprints and other process artifacts, derived from the lower process and function orientation.

CHAPTER 3

Defining the Project/ Program

Defining the project/program (see Figure 3.1) is a key process often neglected or implicit in existing bodies of knowledge. Thanks to a definition of a project or program management activity is grounded, explicit, and can be used for coordination purposes. Defining the project/ program is also a natural by-product of projects or programs as it is reflected by project documentation. So all management products contribute to the definition, which can be treated as project/program evidence. The HybridP3M process of defining the project/program focuses on a stable management environment based on the definition of a project approach, a key document used for consensus.

Adopting HybridP3M Methodology

Project definition involves shaping the project environment for the sake of management and acknowledgment of the uniqueness of an undertaking, characterized by project characteristics. In defining an undertaking as a project or program, it is required to select a methodology first. There exist many ways to manage a project or program, but HybridP3M is the only method that blends traditional management with Agile product delivery based on a sound and thorough approach. It is also distinguished as a holistic approach, combining various project management specializations and subdisciplines. It is both function- and knowledge-oriented based on the ideal of highest maturity levels across organizational dimensions. It is a flexible method based on process adjustments and joint responsibilities for project management processes make it adept in handling complex challenges.

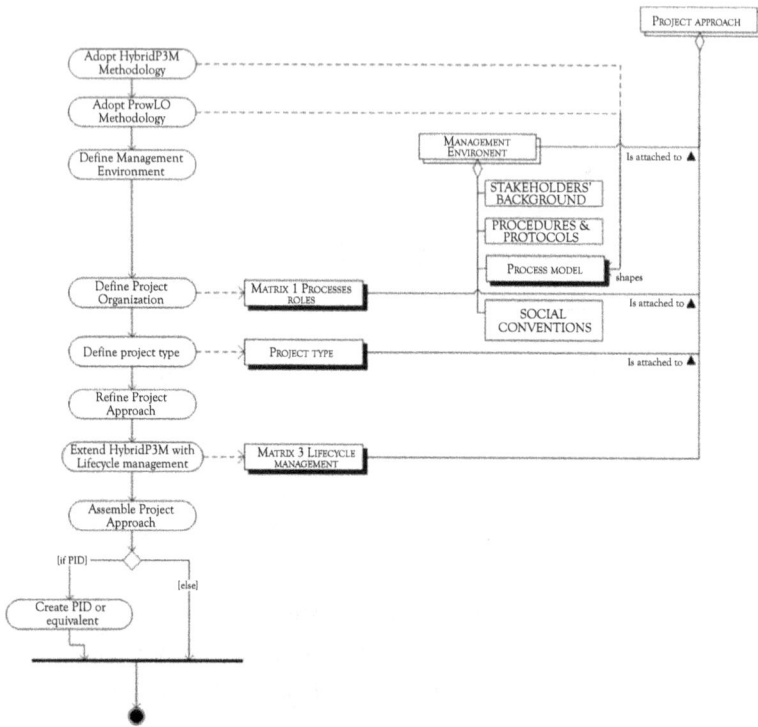

Figure 3.1 Process-Data Diagram of Defining the Project/Program

Adopting ProwLO Methodology

Knowledge management is becoming increasingly recognized as a key factor for project success. In order to achieve project excellence it is an essential process. The project knowledge manager role, typical for HybridP3M, is derived from ProwLO. As such, ProwLO establishes the role of a project knowledge manager, an advocated paradigm shift. Project knowledge management is one of many project management specializations. In adopting the ProwLO methodology, the project or program gains a management framework for knowledge management and thereby support for knowledge processes—essential to business processes. Since ProwLO comprises a unique process model, it partly shapes the management environment, aligned with the project approach in general.

Defining Management Environment

For an effective management of projects and programs, a consensus on the management environment is required. The management environment is an overall view of situational factors that shape processes and affect project outcomes. Accordingly, the definition of management environment makes projects and programs more predictable. The management environment as a defined concept consists of four main elements: (1) stakeholder background, (2) procedures and protocols, (3) process model, and (4) social conventions. The stakeholder background helps to explain routines that may impact project processes. The project management team should identify such routines because stakeholders are influencers and authorities. This type of analysis should take into account preferred project approaches and personal bias. It may reveal knowledge gaps of certain methodologies, methods, and techniques relevant in a project context. Procedures and protocols, usually derived from corporate standards, highly affect project processes. Often they are a given and embedded based on project assurance. It is key that all procedures and protocols do not conflict with the overall process model, the next element. The process model includes HybridP3M's processes, complementary life cycle management (inspired by PRINCE2), and ProwLO's process model. So the overall process model is strongly shaped by methodologies. The process model defines how projects and programs are managed, provided there is compliance. So it is a key concept in process-based project management that gained wide market acceptance, thanks to best practice guides. The final element is social conventions. In any past (like building the great pyramids), current (knowledge era), or foreseeable future era, projects are governed by social conventions. Explicit and implicit assumptions underlying culture impact our understanding of project work and meaning of projects and programs. As a result, without any kind of larger consensus, processes are subject to personal beliefs and group culture. With a better picture of social convention thanks to analysis, project and program management can be put into perspective. This perspective may lead to meta-knowledge (such as the essence behind decision making) and answer many "why" questions (such as why a specific project approach was selected). The practical value of mapping social convention for a greater understanding also relates to international project management where different cultures engage with each other.

Defining Project Organization

An organizational model of the project management team is essential in order to recognize roles and responsibilities. To this end, HybridP3M uses the first matrix that relates HybridP3M processes to roles. Each role represents a specific specialization. Joint responsibilities is a key principle. HybridP3M's agile approach to the project organization eases the burden on project managers greatly. So to define the project organization is essentially to adopt HybridP3M roles and map these to specific processes. The outcome is Matrix 1, which may be tailored to some extent. For example, specific roles like controller and planner can be omitted. In practice, it is also possible to combine roles using a single actor (scaling). In any case the different specializations as distinguished in HybridP3M should be acknowledged and taken as the starting point for any project organization that seeks an agile approach.

Defining the Project Type

To define the project type involves project classification. The added value of this activity resides in the fact that it leads to a better understanding of project work and enables project positioning against industry best practices. As a claimed generic methodology, HybridP3M is most suitable for conventional project and program types. These conventional types are characterized by complexity, often knowledge-intensive work. Also size and risk play a role. Generally, the larger and more risky an undertaking, the greater the need for a holistic and comprehensive approach such as HybridP3M. Small projects with lesser complexity also may benefit from HybridP3M fundamentals, but the additional management overhead needs to be verified and possibly tailored. In the context of defining a project type, it is also helpful to adopt a definition of projects and programs. HybridP3M views both projects and programs as a unique undertaking situated in a complex environment with a clear start, middle, and end and with life cycle characteristics. The distinction between projects and programs is that programs have greater complexity and consist of less coherent program elements, which may or may not be governed as single projects. Programs are usually applied in the case of change initiatives, a complex project type. It should be noted that industry-specific best practices may influence the project approach at various levels.

Instead of introducing a new typology of projects, HybridP3M simply makes a distinction between the following project types:

- ACE (aerospace, construction, engineering)
- Application software development
- Tangible product development
- R&D
- Change (e.g., implementation of software)
- Venture life cycle management (startup, growth, maturity programs)
- Line function projects, single-functional and cross-functional (from mini-undertakings with distinguishable start, middle, and end to more complex tasks with clear role distribution). Note that business as usual is increasingly fading as work is more and more organized around projects.
- Legal projects
- Consultancy assignment
- Business development efforts

Another dimension to project type is the distinction between a commercial customer/supplier environment and a sponsored project/program with internal and/or external stakeholders. The former type of project involves the outsourcing of delivery and/or project management. The latter type of projects is characterized by in-house project execution where corporate management leads or sponsors the initiative. So the procurement model, make-or-buy decisions, determines the project type as well.

Refining the Project Approach

Based on its definition thus far, the project approach needs to be refined and extended with the solution to be developed and method of delivering that solution. The latter provides the foundation for initial planning and ball park estimates. Based on the management environment, Matrix 1, and project type, the refined project approach becomes a relatively stable product. However, it remains subject to change in cases where the solution to be developed is uncertain. The method of delivery, including management framework, is less sensitive to changing requirements.

Extending HybridP3M with Life Cycle Management

Extending HybridP3M with life cycle management adds a time dimension to HybridP3M. This activity involves placing HybridP3M activities in the context of life cycle stages, as captured by, for example, PRINCE2 processes. So the outcome is a mapping between, on the one hand, HybridP3M processes and, on the other hand, PRINCE2 processes. An alternative is the Praxis framework, which also supports life cycle management. This mapping is called Matrix 3, as presented in Chapter 2. Life cycle management acknowledges that projects and programs go through different stages, and that each stage has different requirements. The different stages are characterized by different processes. By extending HybridP3M with life cycle management, it becomes more clear when to execute specific activities. But in HybridP3M, time triggers are of secondary importance. Compliance to HybridP3M processes means functional achievement, which implies adherence to a logical activity flow as captured by a HybridP3M process. When exactly this takes place is not so important, as long as the activity has the right inputs. Accordingly, actors should deal with event triggers related to logical activity flow, that is to say, activity transitions (moving from one activity to another). As projects and programs unfold, management activity also should be planned, as it consumes time and effort. So the overall project plan—to some extent—covers specific activities, reflecting time and event triggers. The planning puts life cycle management into practice.

Assembling a Project Approach

The activity to assemble a project approach is to gather all data in the definition process and combine it into one document. The project approach should always be a formal document, which can be approved by the project board. To summarize, the project approach includes the management environments and its elements, Matrix 1, the project type, Matrix 3, the solution to be delivered, and a summary of the method of delivering that solution (including delivery model). A project approach that has been validated and agreed upon firmly establishes a management framework, which contributes to a stable and predictive management environment.

Creating the PID or Equivalent

In case of a predictive delivery model, it may be an option to invest in an even more comprehensive document than the project approach, as suggested in HybridP3M, namely the creation of a project initiation document (PID). The PID is a formal document as defined in PRINCE2, which requires approval by the project board in order to start project initiation. It contains a lot of data, and similarly to the project approach, it provides a management foundation. Usually, the PID is used as a baseline product in project evaluation, for example, comparing the initial project plan (attached to the PID) with the live project plan. For the specific contents of the PID in PRINCE2, please refer to PRINCE2 guidelines.

Process Aspects

Figure 3.2 captures the knowledge nature of defining a project/program.

$$\bigcirc \text{-2} \quad \bigcirc \text{-1} \quad \circledcirc \text{0} \quad \bigcirc \text{1} \quad \bigcirc \text{2}$$

Figure 3.2 Tacit–explicit continuum of defining a project/program

The type of knowledge involved in defining a project/program is neither predominantly tacit nor explicit. Selecting a project approach over alternatives is based on expert judgment and therefore benefits greatly from tacit experience. In creating Matrix 1 which relates processes to roles, however, explicit knowledge provides the foundation for a mapping, not necessarily the source of tacit experience. Similarly, extending HybridP3M with life cycle management is in essence a combination knowledge conversion mode (explicit to explicit), combining two explicit process models. On the other hand, the exercise is made easier thanks to tacit knowledge gained from experience, while at the same time expert judgement creates a better rationale for the mapping as figured out. In conclusion, depending on a specific definition, knowledge nature is not the best concept to define this process overall.

Figure 3.3 captures the manageability of defining a project/program.

◯ -2 ◉ -1 ◯ 0 ◯ 1 ◯ 2

Figure 3.3 Step-by-step process versus skilled activity continuum of defining a project/program

Ultimately, defining a project/program is more of a kind of step-by-step process than a skilled activity. Based on clear guidelines in combination with templates and examples, project definition is a process that can be repeated without any major problems. The biggest uncertainty stems from selecting the right project approach in the first place. By adopting HybridP3M and ProwLO as two key methodologies, the project approach is to some degree already predetermined. Corporate standards like templates also contribute to standardized documentation. Such factors make this a relatively manageable process. Figure 3.4 captures the specialization level of defining a project/program.

◉ -2 ◯ -1 ◯ 0 ◯ 1 ◯ 2

Figure 3.4 Management–specialist continuum of defining a project/ program

Project/program definition is a typical management process. It involves very limited specialist knowledge. Hence, the most important actor here is the project manager, not any specialist on the management team. Depending on life cycle processes, like startup and initiation, various definition products are created. The project support has a role in this respect. The project board, co-shaping the management environment simply based on role impact, plays a role in externalizing the project approach before capture and documentation. Such externalization would usually take place in the context of discussion moments with the project manager.

Figure 3.5 captures IT support in relation to defining a project/program.

◯ 0 ◯ 1 ◉ 2 ◯ 3 ◯ 4

Figure 3.5 Available IT support for defining a project/program

A key aspect of project/program definition is the adoption of a process model covering any project process rooted in project behavior. There exist solutions on the market that can help promote process models, and thereby provide process support. One available tool is the Method Grid (https://methodgrid.com). Method Grid enables to design, build, and share methods and procedures using two-dimensional grids. An alternative is Insight Intranet HybridP3M Matrix 3 (available on the Insight Intranet platform).

Figure 3.6 captures the complexity of defining a project/program.

◯ 0 ◯ 1 ◉ 2 ◯ 3 ◯ 4

Figure 3.6 Task complexity scale of defining a project/program

The complexity of defining a project/program is best characterized as medium due to the task difficulty. Defining is not just a case of documentation; it is also a matter of selecting, making a case for a project approach, and also a matter of mapping project processes. Given the vast array of potential approaches due to the availability of a large volume of methods, it is most certainly not a trivial task. However, because HybridP3M is considered a holistic approach, the task is made much easier by preselecting HybridP3M as the main methodology to run projects and programs with. On the other hand, the choice for a particular approach has to be rationalized based on arguments and compared against rival approaches. So in any case, this definition process requires a lot of analysis. Sound analysis, in turn, makes an agreed project approach more sensible.

MAIDEO Requirements

Table 3.1 presents MAIDEO requirements related to "defining the project/program."

Table 3.1 MAIDEO *requirements related to defining the project/program*

Requirement	Level	Dimension
There is a well-defined project approach that contributes to a stable management environment.	1	Process and organization
The project approach complements other deliverables, like a PRINCE2 project brief or PID.	1	Process and organization
The project/program has adopted HybridP3M as the core methodology in delivering the anticipated solution.	2	Process and organization
The project/program has adopted ProwLO as the companion methodology for project knowledge management.	2	Process and organization
HybridP3M implementation is not HybridP3M In Name Only, as reflected by actual processes carried out.	3	Process and organization
ProwLO implementation is not ProwLO In Name Only, as reflected by actual knowledge management processes performed.	3	Process and organization
The project/program has adopted life cycle management, extending HybridP3M's functional processes.	3	Process and organization
Project/program definition is recognized as a key subfunction of project management.	4	People and culture
The project approach is assessed in the context of initiating the project for authorization purposes by the project board.	4	Process and organization
The ultimate process model, combining methodologies, methods, and techniques, is promoted using web-based platforms.	5	IT
The management environment subconcept of the project approach is predictive of project behavior, in particular key decisions taken.	5	People and culture

CHAPTER 4

Integrating Knowledge Management

The purpose of integrating knowledge management (see Figure 4.1) is to align HybridP3M with ProwLO guidance. This chapter also covers "integrating knowledge." To support this process the state-of-the-art Knowmadic steps technique is introduced. Knowledge management is becoming increasingly recognized as important to project success.

Organizing KM Brief

In order to integrate knowledge management processes successfully buy-in is required from the project management team as a whole, including the

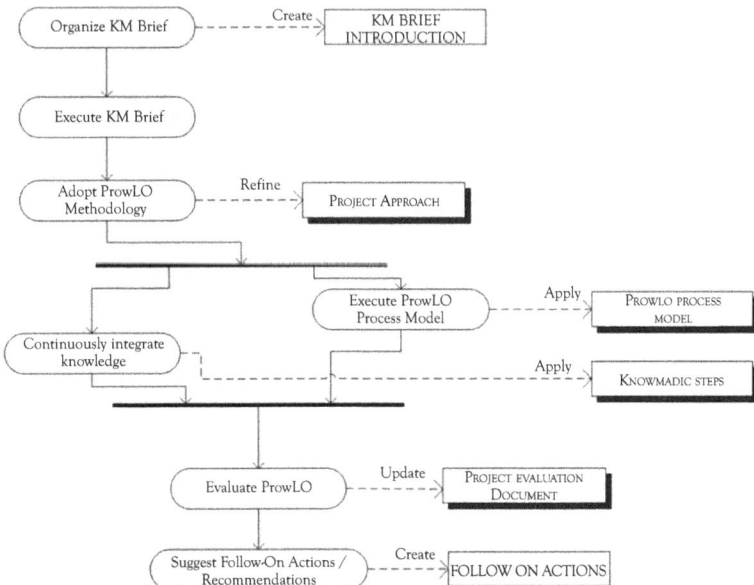

Figure 4.1 Integrating knowledge management PDD

project board. Also awareness from technical specialists is beneficial as knowledge processes reside in all types of work. To this end, the project knowledge manager should organize a KM brief in alignment with the project manager. It is essential that long-term organization knowledge management goals are embedded in the project or program, in addition to conventional project or program goals. The goal of the KM brief is to popularize knowledge management practices, raise awareness, and introduce process implications related to adopting ProwLO, the key project knowledge management methodology. The outcome of this activity is an introduction to knowledge management, which, in practice, could be a PowerPoint presentation.

Executing KM Brief

Once an introduction has been prepared, a meeting with the project management team, project board, and key technical specialists is scheduled and executed. Dialogue and discussion are important aspects. This meeting will foster understanding and acceptance of key knowledge management processes. One specific outcome is the realization that knowledge processes—from knowledge creation to knowledge evolution—affect all people involved in the project, and understanding that a management framework (in the name of ProwLO) is required to facilitate these processes adequately. Facilitating a meeting like the KM brief is mainly people work, requiring people skills, and based on adequate theory to support practices.

Adopting ProwLO Methodology

If formally approved by the project board, in the context of initiating a project or defining a project or program, the ProwLO methodology is adopted as a solution for missing knowledge management processes. There are many roles involved in the application of ProwLO, but the main role is that of the project knowledge manager. He or she is responsible for promoting ProwLO and raising awareness of the role implications for other people on the project management team, project board, and outside of the project/program (situated in other functions of an enterprise), such as, the PMO. ProwLO consists of eight processes, which run in parallel to the PRINCE2 process model (except post-project knowledge control). These processes are designed in such way that knowledge processes are managed effectively and efficiently, taking into consideration knowledge management problems like knowledge/experience gaps, reinventing the wheel, and repeating of mistakes. The importance of ProwLO is based on project as well as organizational benefits. ProwLO enables systematic learning, and therefore, is a condition for optimized processes. Based on ProwLO knowledge and personal experience of key actors, the project approach gets refined. For example, gained from experience, implications of ProwLO are added to the overall project approach.

To adopt the ProwLO methodology in the context of integrating knowledge management is a matter of commitment, not a matter of project or program definition. In the context of project and program definition, the same activity by name is meant to shape the management environment thanks to definition. In this context, however, ProwLO is integrated and internalized by relevant actors in order to successfully execute knowledge management processes as defined in ProwLO.

Executing ProwLO Process Model

The ProwLO manual contains process descriptions, including tables that capture various role implications of the various processes. Armed with this knowledge, the project knowledge manager, supported by the project manager, should be able to execute knowledge management practices in the right manner. Communication with other roles is essential in order to establish social contracts. Knowledge management is not designed to be an isolated process; it requires input from various actors. So process compliance is only one aspect, the other one is to sell knowledge management. For the detailed process model of ProwLO, please see the manual titled *Knowledge Management for Project Excellence.*

Continuously Integrating Knowledge

Continuously integrate knowledge is a parallel activity to "execute ProwLO process model." It involves, on the one hand, validated knowledge with reuse potential, and on the other hand, unvalidated socially generated knowledge. Both cases may include knowledge from projects (newly developed, captured, or gained knowledge). The former type of knowledge demands life cycle support and is the responsibility of the project knowledge manager, taking control of content management. The latter type of knowledge supports team creativity and contributes to expertise status of individual project team members. It also provides a feedback mechanism on validated knowledge fostering knowledge evolution. In order to effectively and efficiently integrate knowledge, of any type, a technique was developed called "Knowmadic steps." This technique is applied in the context of this activity and introduced in the next section.

Knowmadic Steps Technique: Introduction

The Knowmadic steps technique, first conceptualized by Lukasz Rosinski in 2008 as a knowledge structuring approach, comprises five steps in order to integrate knowledge effectively and efficiently (see Figure 4.2). It takes into account specificity of knowledge and utilizes a mechanism to facilitate knowledge distribution, namely a scope and distribution mechanism. This mechanism, and the technique as a whole, is state of the art and a best practice. Knowledge specificity is two-dimensional. The first dimension is project level versus product level, in other words, high level versus low level in terms of scope. The second dimension is project model specific versus project model generic/product specific, in other words, generic or specific knowledge in terms of scope. With regard to the first dimension, the conceptual knowledge needs are either on the project or product level, or a combination. With regard to the second dimension, the conceptual knowledge needs at the project level are either project model specific or project model generic, while the conceptual knowledge needs at the product level are either project model specific or product specific. The difference between "project model generic" and "product specific"—besides the level—is that in case of the former, knowledge objects (at the project level) are generic for all project models within a domain, whereas in case of the latter, knowledge objects related to a particular product are generic for project models that share the product in question (also within a domain). Hence, distribution is dualistic in its essence. The supporting mechanism takes these two dimensions into account.

The first step according to the technique is to make knowledge explicit. This involves knowledge capture, like writing something, or developing knowledge artifacts, which are knowledge container objects. Depending on the type of knowledge and organizational processes, validation may follow.

The second step is to decide whether the knowledge in question is high level or low level. In the context of projects, high level corresponds to the project level, whereas low level corresponds to products. Products, including management and technical products, are a dominant concept in project work and relate to more specific areas of organization and delivery.

The third step is to decide whether the knowledge in question is generic or specific knowledge. This type of assessment relates to how applicable knowledge is in different contexts. It is a measure but practically applied. With regard to the product level, consider, for example, two project models which have a product in common (e.g., a project plan). It is possible that these project models have different templates related to the same product. If that is the case, then we are dealing with knowledge objects that are project model specific—and not product specific. Conversely, other common products of these project models may share particular knowledge objects (implying that they are product specific). The outcome of steps 2 and 3 combined results in a distribution. It should be noted that knowledge objects that are on both the project *and* product level are complex. Such knowledge objects are much less common because it is unusual to have two different scopes at the same time. An important characteristic of such combination is the dependency between the project and product level. The simple rule is that it is not possible to select a project model—in the act of knowledge structuring—that does not have a selected product in common. So there is a strong relationship between the project and product level.

Step 4 is to determine the distribution. Given a universe of domains and project models (types of projects within a bounded domain), the user has to determine the exact distribution. This act depends on how domains and project models are structured. Project model management, a sub-function (of content management) and preliminary work, is the responsibility of the project knowledge manager.

The final step 5 is to distribute the knowledge, digitally, on a corporate knowledge base that takes advantage of the Knowmadic steps technique and associated mechanism for distribution. In the following section, three realistic scenarios are provided to better illustrate practical use.

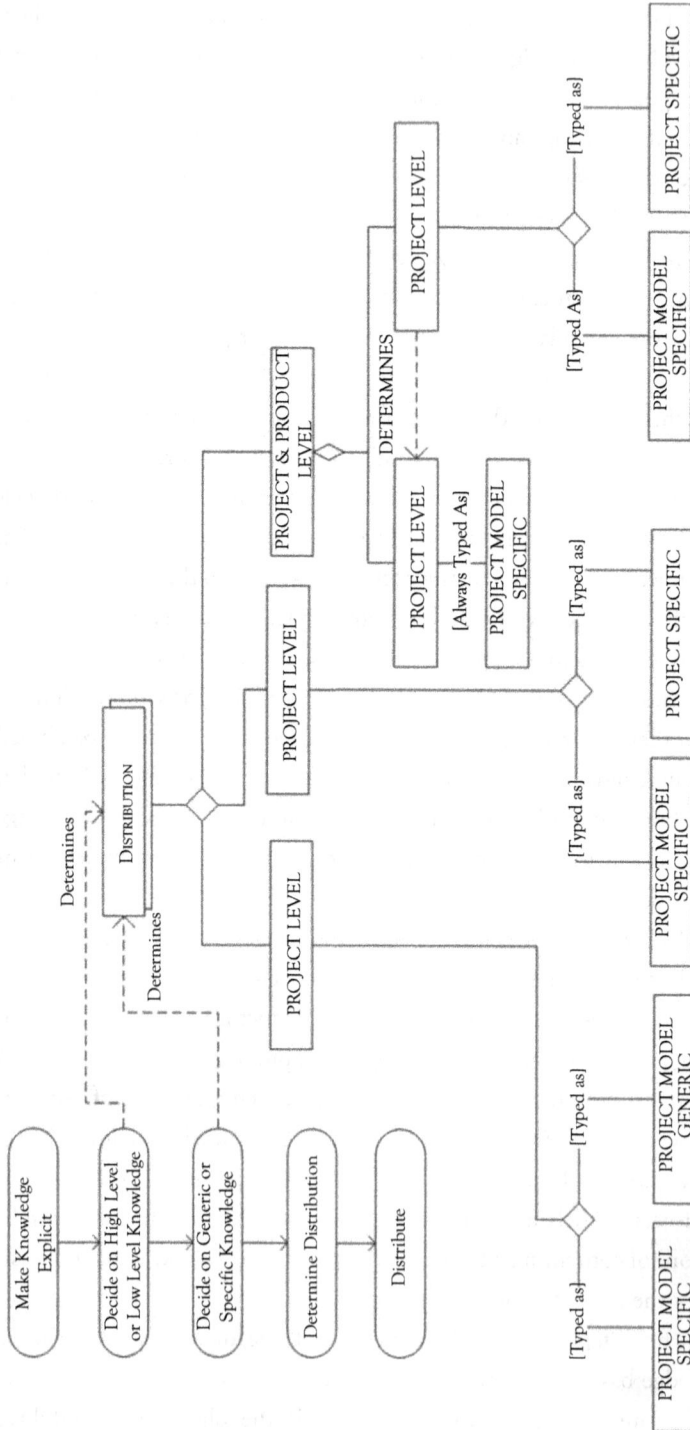

Figure 4.2 Knowmadic steps

The Knowmadic steps technique is performed by the project knowledge manager regarding knowledge objects with claimed reuse potential. These types of knowledge objects are generally files and documents (container knowledge known as tools to support processes). Second, this technique is performed by any project team member regarding socially constructed knowledge in the form of social messages. Regarding the latter, the project knowledge manager should encourage other team members to share knowledge via social messages. An environment characterized by knowledge sharing fosters knowledge creation and development in general.

Applying Knowmadic Steps

The practical application of the Knowmadic steps technique relies on the use of a twofold mechanism for effective and efficient knowledge integration. The following subsections illustrate this mechanism with three examples. Currently, the only software built on this mechanism is KnowledgePlace and the companion platform Insight Intranet.

Project Model Specific Versus Product Specific: The Example of Social Messages

Case A: Project Model-Specific Social Message

Consider a project member who has discovered a best practice from external sources and wants to notify other organizational members—organization-wide—by means of a social message. The claimed best practice is a method (or technique) for the activity of estimating as part of the planning process—in this case the Delphi method (see Wikipedia). However, the appropriateness of a method for estimating depends on the type of project and the present knowledge and experience (Onna and Koning 2002). Taking into account these situational factors, the project member decides that this social message is only relevant for a particular Domain A, and within this domain for three out of four existing project models. Furthermore, he decides that the social message is related to the product of a "project plan." The mechanism to represent this kind of logic in a graphical user interface is shown in Figure 4.3. Note that Product 2 corresponds to the project plan.

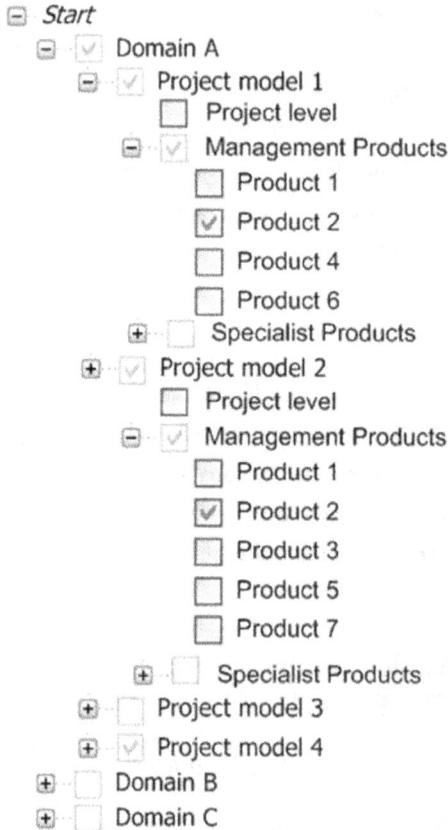

```
⊟ Start
    ⊟ ☑ Domain A
        ⊟ ☑ Project model 1
                 ☐ Project level
            ⊟ ☑ Management Products
                     ☐ Product 1
                     ☑ Product 2
                     ☐ Product 4
                     ☐ Product 6
                ⊞ ☐ Specialist Products
            ⊞ ☑ Project model 2
                 ☐ Project level
            ⊟ ☑ Management Products
                     ☐ Product 1
                     ☑ Product 2
                     ☐ Product 3
                     ☐ Product 5
                     ☐ Product 7
                ⊞ ☐ Specialist Products
            ⊞ ☐ Project model 3
            ⊞ ☑ Project model 4
        ⊞ ☐ Domain B
        ⊞ ☐ Domain C
```

Figure 4.3 Project model specific

Case B: Product-Specific Social Message

The Project Support Office wants to notify organizational members of a recently updated standard template for an issue log in Domain A by means of a social message. In this case, the knowledge object is product specific. In other words, all project models in Domain A that share this product have the same template related to this product. This kind

Start	
⊟ ☑ Domain A	**Project Models in Domain A:**
☐ Project level	*Available:* Project Model 1,2,3,4
	Selected: Project Model 2,3,4
⊟ ☑ Management Products	**Is part of Project Model:**
☐ Product 1	Project Model 1,2,3,4
☐ Product 2	Project Model 1,2,3,4
☑ Product 3	Project Model 2,3,4
☐ Product 4	Project Model 1,3,4
☐ Product 5	Project Model 2,4
☐ Product 6	Project Model 1,4
☐ Product 7	Project Model 2
⊞ ☐ Specialist Products	
⊞ ☐ Domain B	
⊞ ☐ Domain C	

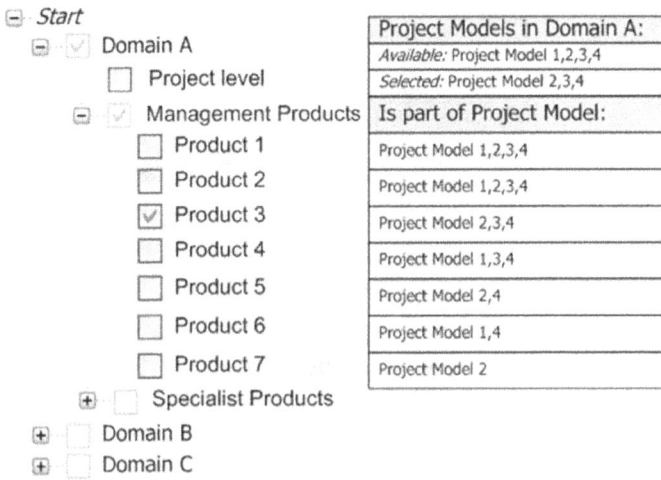

Figure 4.4 Product specific

of logic requires a different mechanism as compared to the previous case (Case A), as presented in Figure 4.4. Note that Product 3 corresponds to an issue log and that not all project models in Domain A have this product in common.

Project and Product Level: The Example of Experiences

It is not unthinkable that a particular knowledge object is on both the project and product level. Consider, for example, a lesson learned related to the project organization. A model of the project organization is not merely one of the many deliverables (i.e., products) of a project; it is an essential part of the project as a whole. Therefore, one may decide that such lesson learned, which is related to the project organization as a product, is also significant at the project level. Furthermore, the lesson learned at the product level is considered as project model specific. The mechanism to represent this kind of logic is based on the mechanism of the first case (Case A) in the previous example and is depicted in Figure 4.5. Note that Product 1 corresponds to the project organization.

⊟ *Start*
  ⊟ ☑ Domain A
    ⊟ ☑ Project model 1
      ☑ Project level
      ⊟ ☑ Management Products
        ☑ Product 1
        ☐ Product 2
        ☐ Product 4
        ☐ Product 6
      ⊞ ☐ Specialist Products
    ⊞ ☑ Project model 2
      ☑ Project level
      ⊟ ☑ Management Products
        ☑ Product 1
        ☐ Product 2
        ☐ Product 3
        ☐ Product 5
        ☐ Product 7
      ⊞ ☐ Specialist Products
    ⊞ ☐ Project model 3
    ⊞ ☐ Project model 4
  ⊞ ☐ Domain B
  ⊞ ☐ Domain C

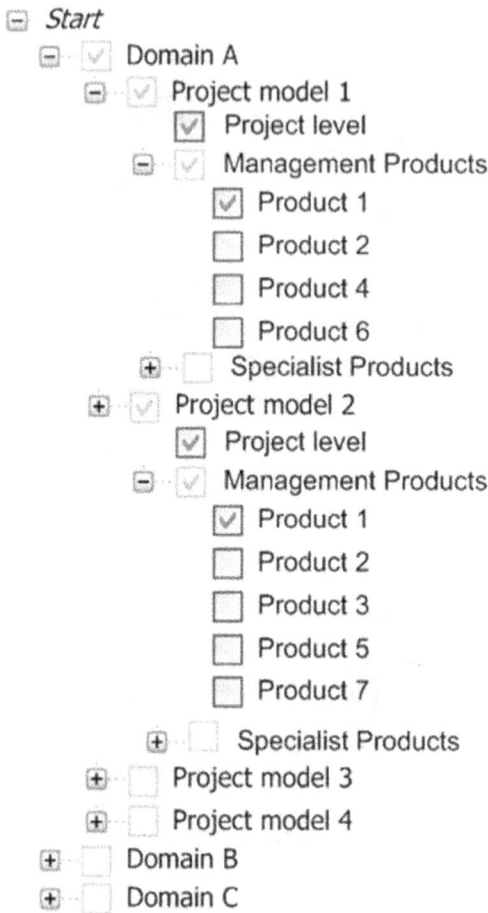

Figure 4.5 Project and product level

Evaluating ProwLO

ProwLO is a complex methodology with deep impact on project processes. At key decision moments and the end of the project the effective use of ProwLO should be evaluated. This involves an analysis of process compliance. At the same time best practices should be established from the viewpoint of various involved actors. The roles and responsibilities elaborated in the ProwLO manual (compressed in tables) provide the foundation for the latter. Evaluation is mainly a responsibility of the project knowledge manager and project manager, but it is recommended to involve other roles as well and everyone on the team has a stake in knowledge management. The analysis should also cover to what extent knowledge needs are satisfied, and hence, input from the team is essential. Realization of organizational benefits that can be accredited to the use or ineffective use of ProwLO should be communicated to the chief knowledge officer or similar by the project knowledge manager, in the form of a report or verbal communication.

Suggesting Follow-On Actions/Recommendations

Following evaluation of ProwLO, the project knowledge manager or project manager should identify follow-on actions/recommendations related to ProwLO. Ideally, ProwLO should evolve into a corporate standard with high process compliance and consistency across projects. In practice, however, a lot depends on the knowledge level of involved actors. So one potential improvement area is sufficient training in the methodology. Change management is also a key aspect. If team members embrace learning, there will be less resistance to ProwLO. As ProwLO does not recommend tailoring and automatically scales (depending on the volume of knowledge needs, project and organizational wise), only minor improvement of the process model itself can be expected, notwithstanding evolution of best practices. However, in practice, depending on the organizational culture and specific organizational problems, some ProwLO processes may become more dominant than others. This is not necessarily a bad thing as long as process goals are recognized and a coherent approach is not compromised.

Process Aspects

Figure 4.6 captures the knowledge nature of integrating knowledge management.

$$\bigcirc \text{-2} \quad \circledcirc \text{-1} \quad \bigcirc \text{0} \quad \bigcirc \text{1} \quad \bigcirc \text{2}$$

Figure 4.6 Tacit–explicit continuum of integrating knowledge management

Integrating knowledge management depends on both explicit and tacit knowledge. For example, in order to execute the ProwLO process a lot of explicit method knowledge is required, as assembled in the ProwLO guide. At the same time, in order to execute ProwLO processes effectively and efficiently tacit knowledge gained from experience is required as well. Similarly, in order to integrate knowledge effectively and efficiently, explicit knowledge about the Knowmadic steps technique is required. But practical experience, and thus tacit knowledge, enables to make the best use of this technique. Overall, tacit knowledge plays arguably a slightly greater role than explicit knowledge in integrating knowledge management.

Figure 4.7 captures the manageability of integrating knowledge management.

$$\bigcirc \text{-2} \quad \bigcirc \text{-1} \quad \bigcirc \text{ 0} \quad \circledcirc \text{1} \quad \bigcirc \text{2}$$

Figure 4.7 Step-by-step process versus skilled activity continuum of integrating knowledge management

Integrating knowledge management is more a skilled activity than step-by-step process. It requires experience and broad knowledge management knowledge. Since knowledge management in the context of projects is a rather new phenomenon, great attention should also be paid to people skills, including the skill to sell or popularize knowledge management. However, since the companion ProwLO methodology is also process based, a lot of knowledge can be reduced to process activity steps, which help to make integrating knowledge management more manageable.

Figure 4.8 captures the specialization level of integrating knowledge management.

$$\bigcirc \text{-2} \quad \bigcirc \text{-1} \quad \bigcirc \text{ 0} \quad \bigcirc \text{1} \quad \circledcirc \text{2}$$

Figure 4.8 Management–specialist continuum of integrating knowledge management

Without any doubt, integrating knowledge management is a specialist process performed by a project knowledge manager. The project knowledge manager is an exceptional role who has both domain knowledge of project management and knowledge management.

Figure 4.9 captures IT support in relation to integrating knowledge management.

$\bigcirc$ 0 $\circledcirc$ 1 $\bigcirc$ 2 $\bigcirc$ 3 $\bigcirc$ 4

Figure 4.9 Available IT support for integrating knowledge management

The only application area of IT in the context of integrating knowledge management is the activity of continuously integrating knowledge. Ideally, IT should support the Knowmadic steps technique like KnowledgePlace. Alternatives to integrating knowledge organization-wide may exist but only the Knowmadic steps technique is state of the art, for the best kind of knowledge integration, most effective and efficient.

Figure 4.10 captures the complexity of integrating knowledge management.

$\bigcirc$ 0 $\bigcirc$ 1 $\bigcirc$ 2 $\bigcirc$ 3 $\circledcirc$ 4

Figure 4.10 Task complexity scale of integrating knowledge management

The complexity of integrating knowledge management can be evidenced by various means. For example, the ProwLO methodology is very complex. For example, there is a natural tension between ordinary project management with short-term goals and long-term knowledge management, each demanding time and resources. Knowledge management in the context of projects is recently understood but not yet widely practiced. Also the Knowmadic steps technique is quite complex—at least it may appear to be abstract—at first sight and requires some learning for personal knowledge mastery.

MAIDEO Requirements

Table 4.1 lists MAIDEO requirements related to integrating knowledge management.

Table 4.1 **MAIDEO** *requirements related to integrating knowledge management*

Requirement	Level	Dimension
The project organization has a designated project knowledge manager role.	1	Process and organization
The project knowledge manager is ProwLO certified.	1	People and culture
The project management team is familiar with ProwLO.	2	People and culture
The project knowledge manager applies ProwLO processes from the ProwLO process model.	2	Process and organization
The project board promotes knowledge management.	2	People and culture
The ProwLO process model is consistently applied across projects and programs.	3	Process and organization
The project team shares knowledge via social messages.	3	People and culture
ProwLO is established as a corporate standard.	4	Process and organization
ProwLO compliance is assessed in the context of project assurance.	4	Process and organization
Organization uses Knowmadic steps software.	5	IT
The project knowledge manager is content manager for project knowledge.	5	IT

CHAPTER 5

Planning

Planning follows expectations (see Figure 5.1). It is often part of contractual agreements in case of predictive delivery. Planning is a very traditional concept that needs to be adjusted with the delivery model, either predictive or agile. HybridP3M's approach to planning is characterized by very explicit planning objectives, the commonly used work breakdown structure (WBS), and planning iterations with or without baselines, depending on the delivery model. The planning iterations focus on the planning of Work Packages aligned with Agile product delivery. HybridP3M also introduces the concept of "project history plan," a plan that emerges based on actual progress and hindsight information. The project history plan is more dominant in Agile delivery, which is less predictable and thus more difficult to plan. The project history plan is very useful for evaluation purposes and learning across projects.

Defining and Analyzing Product

The first step in the planning process is always to define and analyze the product. The outcome is a product definition, and thus, this activity also relates to project/ program definition. The product definition defines the end product, and likely subcomponents or features. The delivery of an end product is usually organized around key deliverables for control and handover purposes. Analysis of the product helps to define these key deliverables. In practice, make-or-buy decisions determine whether specific components are external, third-party products. Such external products, adopted from PRINCE2, should be designated as such in the planning process, and require special attention given the additional uncertainty factor (e.g., regarding the delivery process or quality). Finally, the product definition is added to the "overall project plan."

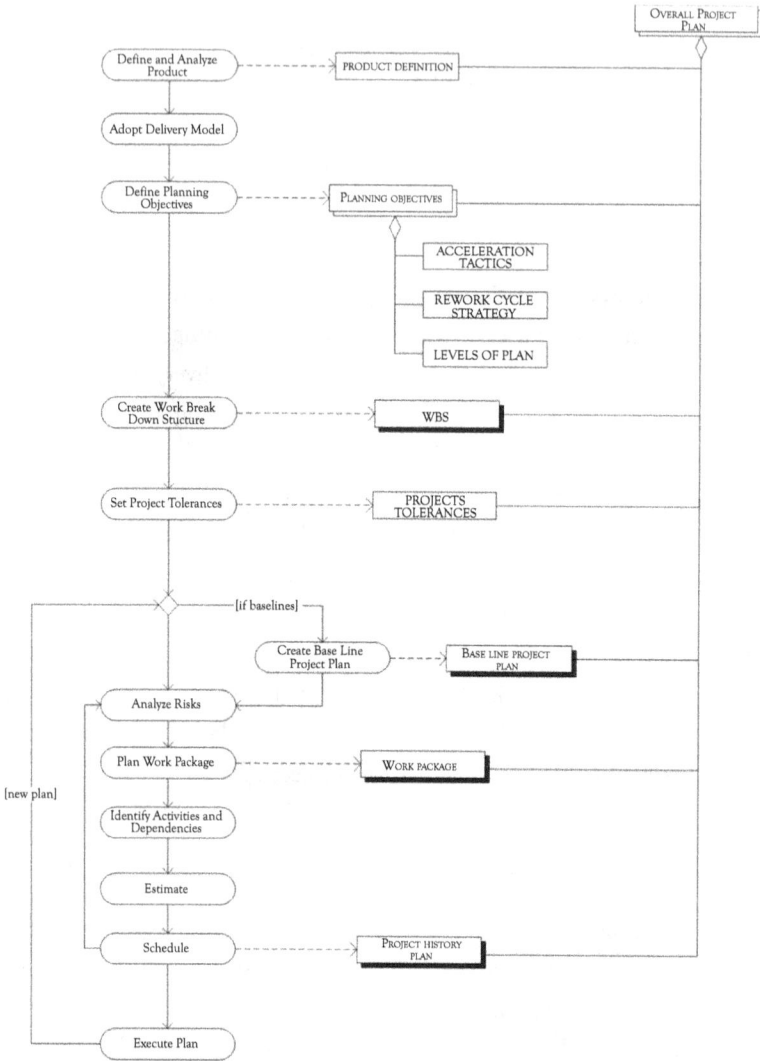

Figure 5.1 Planning PDD

Adopting Delivery Model

The second step in the planning process is to choose a delivery model. HybridP3M is compatible with both Agile and waterfall delivery. The HybridP3M process of Agile product delivery is essentially an agile approach. However, the stage-gate paradigm applies as well. So a waterfall approach based on linear stages is possible as well. It should be noted that selecting a particular delivery model is binary: it is either waterfall or agile. Something in between does not exist. So a hybrid methodology like HybridP3M is not something in between either. HybridP3M simply combines Agile product delivery, being compatible with waterfall as well, with traditional management control as overhead for more predictive behavior.

Defining Planning Objectives

The third step is to define planning objectives. A distinction can be made between at least three types of planning objectives: (1) acceleration tactics, (2) rework cycle strategy, and (3) levels of plan. Acceleration tactics refer to tactical decisions, like for example,parallel planning of activities, that aim to reduce project duration. Acceleration can be desirable from the outset but also when projects fall behind schedule due to various reasons. With acceleration comes greater risk. One perverse outcome of acceleration could be the increase of rework. Rework cycles, which often lay at the root of disruption and delay, should be considered at a strategic level in combination with acceleration tactics, especially in case of Agile delivery due to changing requirements. There are potentially three levels of plan: at the project level, stage level, and team level (adopted from PRINCE2). The delivery model has great impact on the levels of plan. In case of Agile delivery, the project level plan is less detailed and no stage or team plans are guiding material. In case of waterfall delivery, the project plan is detailed and controlled based on lower-level stage plans. In case of large waterfall projects with multiple teams, team plans add value thanks to even greater detail.

Creating Work Breakdown Structure

The next step is to create a WBS, a hierarchical structure of elements that comprise the end product. PRINCE2 uses a product breakdown structure focused on products and subproducts. HybridP3M uses the more widely known WBS. The difference is that the WBS focuses on activity, related to deliverables or project outcomes, a nuance as such. A WBS is the preferred notion, especially when dealing with less tangible products, like services or change. The creation of a WBS is a skill and rather self-explanatory. Knowledge such as examples of similar past projects is very useful to this end.

Setting Planning Tolerances

Based on the overall business case, planning tolerances are needed as a control mechanism. Exceeding such tolerances—anticipated or actually—triggers management-by-exception, the situation in which decision makers decide on the viability of the project while handling the exception, based on intervention such as corrective actions or adjusted tolerances. Since HybridP3M is based on Agile product delivery, stage tolerances cannot be applied, only tolerances at the project level, associated with the fundamental business case. Planning tolerances cover not only time, in order to deliver just-in-time, but also resources like human resources as well as budget required for the investment (on-budget). Scope is another possible tolerance as to limit or exclude certain functionality based on early premises. Tolerances are usually set in percentages based on ball park estimates in combination with required or desired outcomes, such as in terms of duration.

Creating Baseline Project Plan

A baseline project plan is an optional element, depending on the delivery model. In case of predictive delivery such as waterfall, a baseline project plan is used for evaluation and control purposes. A baseline project plan is a plan at the *project* level. This means that the level of detail is limited. The contents usually would reflect the ball park estimates, given a high-level WBS. The plan is further characterized by distinct stages, which are project phases ending with decision moments to continue with the next stage, in other words, go-no-go decisions. The additional schedule is handy for monitoring progress. For example, predictive projects and programs can benefit from the earned value management technique. In the context of evaluation, project deviations are closely examined by comparing actual plans against the baseline project plan. This type of analysis helps to answer project performance. Since HybridP3M is a generic method, also applicable to an Agile context, stage plan baselines are omitted. The Agile context is too dynamic for predictive stages, but not to the extent that stages cannot be identified at all, provided that project outcomes are not unknown. Extreme projects where requirements are uncertain or unknown not only lack baseline project plans, but lack a project planning process as we know it. The following activities focus on smaller chunks of the project plan organized around Work Packages. In a generic context, Work Packages define stages and should be planned for Agile product delivery.

Analyzing Risks

The activity to analyze risks initially follows the development of a baseline project plan. Based on the latter, risks can be identified related to planning. Many planning risks are related to productivity losses and the rework cycle (Eden et al. 2000), which contribute to the cost of disruption and delay. For example, a subcontractor might fail to deliver a needed product on time, or a resource may not perform at the required level. On occasion, external events may create a crisis, disrupting timely delivery of several products. Analyze risks is a recurring activity as part of new iterations triggered by the need for planning new Work Packages. As new information on new Work Packages becomes available, the planner, supported by the risk manager (or vice versa), may identify new risks or update existing risks. Analyze risks always follows the incentive to plan a Work Package, preceding Work Package definition and planning (as depicted in the diagram) or, alternatively, should at least run in parallel. Given a record of risks, planning the Work Package can be adjusted so that risks are mitigated.

Planning Work Package

The activity to plan Work Packages is typical for hybrid project management, having roots in traditional project management. The concept of Work Package is compatible with Agile because delivery always needs to be defined and planned, and Work Packages are suitable for this purpose. Agile sprints, an Agile notion for fast delivery of manageable chunks, would imply at least one Work Package, but more are possible. Also many organizations have IT systems that record Work Packages for supplier purposes, which link work with costs, and thus, the invoicing process in a commercial customer/supplier environment. A Work Package is essentially a summary of the work that needs to be carried out. It covers a set of requirements and, in case of product-based planning, a specific product description (referring to deliverables), and associates with a specific stage and possibly multiple user stories (in software development).

Identifying Activities and Dependencies

The activity of identifying activities and dependencies consists of two steps: (1) identify all activities required to deliver the products (including project management products) and (2) determine interdependencies between activities. During the second step, one should take into account both internal and external dependencies (e.g., delivery of an external product or decision from corporate/program management). In case of other project outcomes, alternative to products, such as change or capability, activities are identified that support those outcomes. The WBS is used as input and further elaborated with additional detail. PRINCE2 also uses a project flow diagram that can be used in the context of this activity.

Estimating

Once all activities have been identified, the next step is to make estimates. Estimates relate to work, usually in man hours; duration, based on available resources assigned to activities; and cost, which follows work. Estimating is essential for control of cost and duration, and the notion of progress. It is of utmost importance that estimates are accurate for realistic scheduling, the following step. In many industries there exist specific techniques for estimating. The most common and generic technique is expert judgment. A subtechnique in this respect is capacity planning, which states that x available resources result in y duration. Another common technique is analogy, which presumes that similar projects account for similar estimates. This requires systematic registration of projects, according to specific attributes and project types, classification in general. Furthermore, in the software industry parametric models have been applied, in which parameters determine estimates. Parametric techniques use an algorithm and also take into account historic data. In case of software development, one example is to calculate estimates based on the number of functions required in code. Functions relate to specific requirements. This is called function-point analysis, and there exist a number of variations. Another example of a parametric technique is COCOMO.

Scheduling

According to PRINCE2, a plan is a comprehensive management product describing what is required, how and when this will be achieved, and by whom. Visually, this information can be captured by a schedule such as a Gantt chart. Essentially, a schedule is a list of activities and their allocated resources, plus dates over which the activities take place. As most people think of plans as charts with time scales (according to official guidance), such visual representations play a central role in plans. With every new Work Package planned, the overall schedule is modified. This overall schedule is the main element of the project history plan, a new management product introduced in HybridP3M. In other words, the live schedule provides the source for this product. The project history plan depicts progress based on actual statistics. In an Agile context, this product is very valuable because it provides essential input for project evaluation as baselines cannot be used for this purpose.

Executing Plan

Supported by schedules, plans are executed. Executing a plan is the actual work managed according to a delivery process. HybridP3M's delivery process is introduced in Chapter 16.

Process Aspects

Figure 5.2 captures the knowledge nature of planning.

$$\bigcirc \text{-2} \quad \bigcirc \text{-1} \quad \bigcirc \text{ 0} \quad \circledcirc \text{1} \quad \bigcirc \text{2}$$

Figure 5.2 Tacit–explicit continuum of planning

Planning mainly relies on explicit planning information. Only explicit knowledge can facilitate agreement on planning. The only tacit dimension of planning (arguably) is the activity to estimate, provided this involves expert judgment.

Figure 5.3 captures the manageability of planning.

$$\bigcirc \text{-2} \quad \circledcirc \text{-1} \quad \bigcirc \text{0} \quad \bigcirc \text{1} \quad \bigcirc \text{2}$$

Figure 5.3 Step-by-step process versus skilled activity continuum of planning

Planning is essentially a step-by-step process that can be rationalized and standardized. To a certain extent it does build on skilled activity, but this is limited to the right use of supporting tools (i.e., it depends on system knowledge). So corporate standards are ideal for promoting and managing the planning process.

Figure 5.4 captures the specialization level of planning.

$$\bigcirc \text{-2} \quad \bigcirc \text{-1} \quad \bigcirc \text{0} \quad \circledcirc \text{1} \quad \bigcirc \text{2}$$

Figure 5.4 Management–specialist continuum of planning

Planning is rather a specialization. While most project managers can create planning schedules, which is key planning data, mature organizations use specialist planners. For example, it takes experience to understand interdependencies integrated in plans or the impact of risk on project planning. Also, planning is closely tied with monitoring and control. This may imply some basic understanding of techniques such as earned value management, complementing planning with progress control.

Figure 5.5 captures IT support in relation to planning.

$$\bigcirc \text{0} \quad \bigcirc \text{1} \quad \bigcirc \text{2} \quad \bigcirc \text{3} \quad \circledcirc \text{4}$$

Figure 5.5 Available IT support for planning

Of all project subfunctions, planning is the most popular area for IT support. There is an abundance of project planning software on the international market. MS Project is one of the most popular tools, but there are plenty of alternatives. The list would go on, with large players and smaller ones.

Figure 5.6 captures the complexity of panning.

$$\bigcirc 0 \quad \bigcirc 1 \quad \bigcirc 2 \quad \bullet 3 \quad \bigcirc 4$$

Figure 5.6 Task complexity scale of planning

Planning is rather a complex process. Even more so in Agile projects with a smaller planning horizon. Ultimately, the effectiveness of planning and the usefulness of schedules (a key point of planning) depend on accurate estimates. The complex WBSs are also invaluable. Aspects such as acceleration and risk awareness make planning more complicated or complex.

MAIDEO Requirements

Table 5.1 presents MAIDEO requirements related to "planning."

Table 5.1 MAIDEO requirements related to planning

Requirement	Level	Dimension
The product is defined and analyzed.	1	Organization and process
The selected delivery model aligned with planning is treated as a binary choice.	1	Organization and process
External products are considered in the planning process.	2	Organization and process
The project uses schedules for the coordination of planned activity.	2	Monitoring and control
The project uses a basic work breakdown structure or equivalent product breakdown structure.	2	Organization and process
Planning objectives include a reference to acceleration tactics, the rework cycle, and address levels of plan.	3	Organization and process
Planning tolerances are applied.	3	Monitoring and control
In predictive delivery baselines plans are used for evaluation and control.	3	Monitoring and control
Risks are integrated with planning and considered on a continuous basis.	4	Organization and process
Planning involves Work Packages.	4	Organization and process
Advanced specialist estimation techniques are applied.	5	Organization and process
Both internal and external interdependencies are addressed in the planning process.	5	Organization and Process

CHAPTER 6

Risk Management

Risk management is a specialism and continuous process as projects and programs unfold (see Figure 6.1). The effectiveness of a risk management process highly depends on the ability to identify risks in the first place. So historical data on similar projects is useful to this end, together with the ability to detect threat. Risk management has been covered extensively in the literature, contributing to the wealth of knowledge. What characterizes HybridP3M's risk management process is a simple, at a high-level linear process that takes into account the implications of countermeasures (based on causality) by addressing interdependencies and adjustments. This approach is rooted in decision making and cause and effect, or simply project behavior, as outlined by the Cases method, which captures problem + solution scenarios (Rosinski 2019). The basic assumption is that the impact of countermeasures can be anticipated based on foresight, enabling adjustments based on decision implications. And secondly, that the actual impact of countermeasures is to a degree uncertain, with unprecedented implications due to unexpected project behavior, that is, nonobvious cause and effects. Essentially, risk management involves a decision-making process driven by the need for risk mitigation.

Identify Risks

The first step is to identify risks. Risks capture all things that can go wrong or not as expected. It takes a creative mind and (negative) experience to identify such phenomena. Every risk identified as one is usually a summary of a risk, captured in one line, for the purpose of brevity, which needs to be elaborated and explained. So the contextual information of risk is important as well. While the roots of risk are unlimited, it may be possible to categorize risk, for example, based on taxonomies. Such categorization can arguably make the search for risks easier. A common

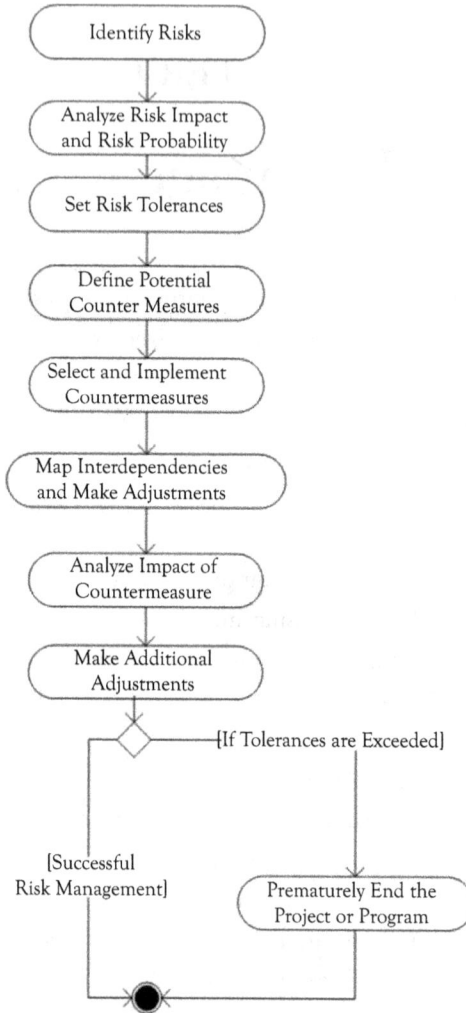

Figure 6.1 Risk management PDD

divide is risks common to the business/industry in general and risks specific to an organization, for example, rooted in certain product characteristics—either penetrating an existing market or new market development, depending on differentiation. Examples of risks in case of new online venture, combined with new product development, a complex change initiative, include entry of new competitors, online user growth does not meet expectations, no loan from the bank, bullying by copyright/ trademark owners, low conversion to premium (paid) accounts, launch of substitutes, and so on. One example of an existing taxonomy is the one that follows the RISMAN method, in which there are seven perspectives relevant to risk: (1) political/governance, (2) financial/economical, (3) legal, (4) technical, (5) organizational, (6) geographical, and (7) societal.

Analyze Risk Impact and Risk Probability

The second step is to analyze risk impact and risk probability, using easy to use scales. Risk impact refers to the consequences of risk once it materializes (the actual damage), whereas risk probability refers to the likelihood a risk materializes. This type of analysis makes it possible to prioritize focus. It provides the risk manager a tool to prioritize related countermeasures, identified at a later stage, as well. Performing step 2, following step 1, will result in a standardized table. In this table, every identified risk gets an ID and assessment of risk impact and risk probability. The most common scale is low–medium–high. Obviously, if impact or probability is high, or a combination, then the associated risks should receive great attention.

Set Risk Tolerances

Risk tolerance is the degree of how much of a risk one is willing to take. More specifically, for each specific risk, partly defined by risk impact and risk probability, risk tolerance is the degree of accepting risk without planning and implementing countermeasures. Accepting risk is effectively a function of risk impact and risk probability, and thus, it relates to risk impact and risk probability. So if these two variables change based on new insight thanks to dynamic risk analysis and risk tolerance does not, then either countermeasures are required or a new level of risk tolerance. From a proactive stance, risk tolerance also depends on potential countermeasures. If risk can be mitigated by potential countermeasures effectively, this will justify risk tolerance. In other words, if things go wrong, the negative impact can be minimized. This point of view provides a new meaning to risk tolerance as a function of countermeasure effectiveness, in addition to risk impact and risk probability. The latter extended meaning of risk tolerance relies on identification of *potential* countermeasures, which is the next step anyway.

Define Potential Countermeasures

For every identified risk, HybridP3M recommends to define one or more potential countermeasures. Such countermeasures either limit risk impact or risk probability, or a combination. In other words, countermeasures either mitigate negative effects in case risk materializes or prevent risk from materializing in the first place. Every defined potential countermeasure should be feasible in alignment with the current situation. Also, every countermeasure has innate advantages and disadvantages, depending on the countermeasure impact, which are worth recording.

Select and Implement Countermeasures

Not every identified potential countermeasure needs to be implemented. This depends on factors such as risk priority and countermeasure effectiveness. So there is a step that involves the selection of countermeasures ready for implementation. While risk management is a specialism performed by the risk manager, decision making affecting the project or program as a whole—with serious consequences/impact—involves project manager authority or even project board authority. So this step is a joint responsibility of the risk manager and project manager, who may escalate an issue to the project board in the spirit of the decision-making process, especially when project tolerances are under threat. After selection of countermeasures ready to be implemented—following decision making—the implementation process starts. Implementation requires project manager authority and involves change to the project management environment, project management processes, or delivery processes. So every selected countermeasure may benefit from change management, essentially a leadership process delegated over project management roles, *not* a separate project management function according to HybridP3M. Note that a change manager role is a specialist role dealing with project outcomes, especially in case of change initiatives.

Map Interdependencies and Make Adjustments

The implementation of selected countermeasures should trigger analysis of interdependencies, either prior to implementation or in the act itself, setting project behavior in motion. The project management environment subject to various internal and external, management, and specialist processes could be regarded as a complex system. Changes to this system based on corrective measures related to risk management undoubtedly influence project behavior, either in a negative, positive, or neutral way (but often with managerial implications). The key is to control project behavior in such a way that it does not conflict with desired project outcomes, including project results, nor jeopardize project success as viewed by project stakeholders. Therefore, it is essential to map interdependencies of implemented countermeasures in order to better understand the system as a whole for the benefit of prediction and management control. A best practice in this type of analysis is to analyze the measure's impact on every single project/program and P3M function. Recall that HybridP3M's processes are directly derived from functions. Accordingly, it is recommended to develop additional tools such as checklists to see how countermeasures affect the relevant functions. Following a mapping of selected countermeasures and interdependencies, adjustments need to be made. These adjustments relate to the aforementioned functions, such as project planning, various assumptions at the foundation of the project or program (e.g., tolerances, business case, and market knowledge), and the project management environment in general. Making these adjustments will likely affect project management processes and requires alignment with other persons taking responsibility for process and role. For example, if a specific countermeasure implies purposeful delay, affecting project planning, the project planner may require a new planning tolerance in order to prevent an exception, and thus, more project board intervention.

Analyze Impact of Countermeasure

Every implemented countermeasure follows a decision-making process leading to action. Taken decision and actions combined correspond to a human response to a problem. Risk management problems, called risks, pose an initial problem that might be dealt with countermeasures on the outset. Hence, risk management can be approached by a decision making and project behavior inducing paradigm, the foundation behind the Cases method (Rosinski 2019). What can be learned from this specific paradigm is that there are feedback loops inherent to management events. There is a distinction between what is expected and what actually happens, the outcome of decision making. So in order to solve the initial problem, additional actions may be required. Or the initial problem evolves into different problem or set of problems, calling for alternative action. Therefore, in practice, risk management may lead to unexpected project behavior. Accordingly, it is the task of the risk manager to analyze the impact of countermeasures over a course of time. This will enable understanding of the new situation, the effectiveness of taken countermeasures, and may lead to better decision making in the next iteration of the problem (risk) situation. The next iteration(s) of solving the risk calls for the next step: "Make additional adjustments."

Make Additional Adjustments

Based on risk status, as it evolves over time, one may conclude impact of countermeasures and thereby acknowledge the end of iteration. Every iteration is characterized by project behavior in terms of actual outcome, as the result of taken decision and actions, in this case, risk countermeasures. Actual outcome may reflect changes to risk impact, risk probability, or simply risk resolution in which risk is no longer actual. The actual outcome may trigger additional countermeasures, which are additional adjustments. The process is potentially iterative, depending on risk complexity, selecting a particular countermeasure and emergent factors. These factors all contribute to unexpected project behavior, and thus, unanticipated actual outcomes. The advantage of this iterative approach to risk management is that in most cases it will lead to successful resolution of risk thanks to implementation of effective countermeasures. If risk cannot be resolved and at the same time cannot be tolerated, the situation may result in a premature end of the project or program, as decided by project board members. In order to capture risk management knowledge for future reference, it is recommended to apply the Cases method introduced by Rosinski (2019). The Cases method is a decision-making tool for problems and can be used for risk.

Prematurely End the Project or Program

If the original risk countermeasure or follow-up countermeasures (in case of iterative problem solving) are effective, either resolve the risk or lead to intelligent risk tolerance, then one can speak of successful risk management. The opposite case of unresolved risk can lead to a premature end of the project or program, depending on risk tolerance. Risk tolerance is established by the project board and affects the business case. If risk is not tolerable, the project board may conclude that the project or program is not worthwhile. So risk partly determines viability. Arguably, many projects or programs fail because they lack a sound risk management process. Such process helps to resolve risk, or in case that is no longer an option, it provides a safeguard against sunk costs (when simply ending the project or program is the best option). That is to say, such projects and programs carry on based on the wrong premises, rooted in a faulty business case.

Process Aspects

Figure 6.2 captures the knowledge nature of risk management.

$$\bigcirc \text{-2} \quad \bigcirc \text{-1} \quad \circledcirc \text{0} \quad \bigcirc \text{1} \quad \bigcirc \text{2}$$

Figure 6.2 Tacit–explicit continuum of risk management

While risk capture results in explicit risk, risk management also involves tacit knowledge. Risk mitigation based on countermeasures is a problem-solving paradigm which depends on tacit knowledge of countermeasure effectiveness. Also risk analysis in terms of risk impact and risk probability has tacit dimensions. Overall, risk management contributes to explicit knowledge on risk and its management.

Figure 6.3 captures the manageability of risk management.

$$\bigcirc \text{-2} \quad \circledcirc \text{-1} \quad \bigcirc \text{0} \quad \bigcirc \text{1} \quad \bigcirc \text{2}$$

Figure 6.3 Step-by-step process versus skilled activity continuum of risk management

The process of mitigating risks is a manageable process consisting of clear, nonambiguous steps. Risk management can be effectively promoted based on corporate standards. Although it is a specialization rooted in a unique knowledge domain, it is not a specialization that requires difficult to copy skills, relatively speaking. In other words, the systematic approach behind risk management is relatively easy to grasp, except the essence of decision making relevant in this context.

Figure 6.4 captures the specialization level of risk management.

$$\bigcirc \text{-2} \quad \bigcirc \text{-1} \quad \bigcirc \text{0} \quad \circledcirc \text{1} \quad \bigcirc \text{2}$$

Figure 6.4 Management–specialist continuum of risk management

As mentioned earlier, risk management is a specialization. Depending on the project or program, the distinct risk manager role is combined with the project manager role (or there is no awareness of a separate role). Generally, project managers should understand risk management and acknowledge its importance. So the mentioned combination is not something far-fetched. In fact, although propagated by HybridP3M, a separate risk manager role is not common practice across industries in the present state.

Figure 6.5 captures IT support in relation to risk management.

$$\bigcirc \text{0} \quad \circledcirc \text{1} \quad \bigcirc \text{2} \quad \bigcirc \text{3} \quad \bigcirc \text{4}$$

Figure 6.5 Available IT support for risk management

Maybe surprisingly the market offers a significant number of risk management tools. Surprisingly because risk management can be performed using simple Excel sheets at most. Clearly, available software builds upon the analytical dimension of risk. The tools in the market effectively combine risk data and display information in the style of either reports or some kind of dashboards. Generally, the goal of these tools is to support monitoring of risk. Also, some tools enable intelligent aggregation of risk data.

Figure 6.6 captures the complexity of risk management.

$\bigcirc$ 0 $\bigcirc$ 1 $\circledcirc$ 2 $\bigcirc$ 3 $\bigcirc$ 4

Figure 6.6 Task complexity scale of risk management

As a process, risk management is rather straightforward. But the decision-making dimension makes it more complex. Risk has a big impact on projects and programs, so risk mitigation calls for deliberation and sound decision making.

MAIDEO Requirements

Table 6.1 presents MAIDEO requirements related to "risk management."

Table 6.1 MAIDEO requirements related to risk management

Requirement	Level	Dimension
Risks are identified as part of the business case	1	Organization and process
Risks are categorized using simple taxonomies	1	Organization and process
Risk analysis takes into account risk impact and risk probability	2	Organization and process
Risk tolerances are established for each major risk	2	Organization and process
The decision-making process regarding countermeasures is a joint responsibility of the risk manager and project manager	3	Organization and process
Implemented countermeasures are supported in the organization	3	People and culture
The implementation of countermeasures follows change management principles	4	Organization and process
Prior to implementing countermeasures, interdependencies are mapped for possible additional adjustments	4	Organization and process
The impact of countermeasures is monitored and evaluated properly	5	Monitoring and control
Risk assessment can result in a premature end of the project or program; it is not being neglected in key decision making	5	Monitoring and control

CHAPTER 7

Business Case Development

Business cases justify investment of capital, resources, and time for the delivery of something new or change (see Figure 7.1). They are a justification control mechanism for the project board with the potential to end a project or program lifecycle. Business cases are also a key information need of corporate and portfolio management as project or program benefits add value to the business of an organization and therefore its success and survival. In the context of projects or programs, the business case is essentially a tool to determine the viability of undertakings. In the context of the organization, the senior responsible owner (a term used by AXELOS) is responsible for initiating independent assurance reviews of business case viability (Brolsma and Kouwenhoven 2019). Based on the latter, corporate or portfolio management may intervene top-down and overrule that part of the project board, which represents corporate interests—a P3M process interface. In practice, the executive (who represents the company's business case) then has to comply with such intervention. Note that the executive project role is one out of three PRINCE2 project board roles (next to senior user and senior supplier), but in reality project boards can be composed differently depending on stakeholder interests. It is no mystique that the business case of projects and programs needs to be tailored based on organizational needs. This is an exception in HybridP3M. Like explained in the Introduction, tailoring methods based on parameters like project characteristics is a mystique (or wishful thinking), but here tailoring is driven by company-specific requirements, often depending on financial systems. As a process, business case development comprises activities that add new information to the business case as a whole. It is a dynamic process as projects and programs unfold because assumptions need to be constantly tested, and in practice they change quite often. So the business case is dynamic. Note that the definition of the business case helps to define project or program success in the evaluation process. The contents proposed by HybridP3M are based on market knowledge and comply with our general understanding of business cases. The specific interpretation of the various elements however is unique to some extent.

Provide Background Information

A formal business case should always include background information, usually corresponding to the reasons or triggers behind the project or program. Essentially, background information captures the significance of a project or program in plain words, starting with the assessment of the

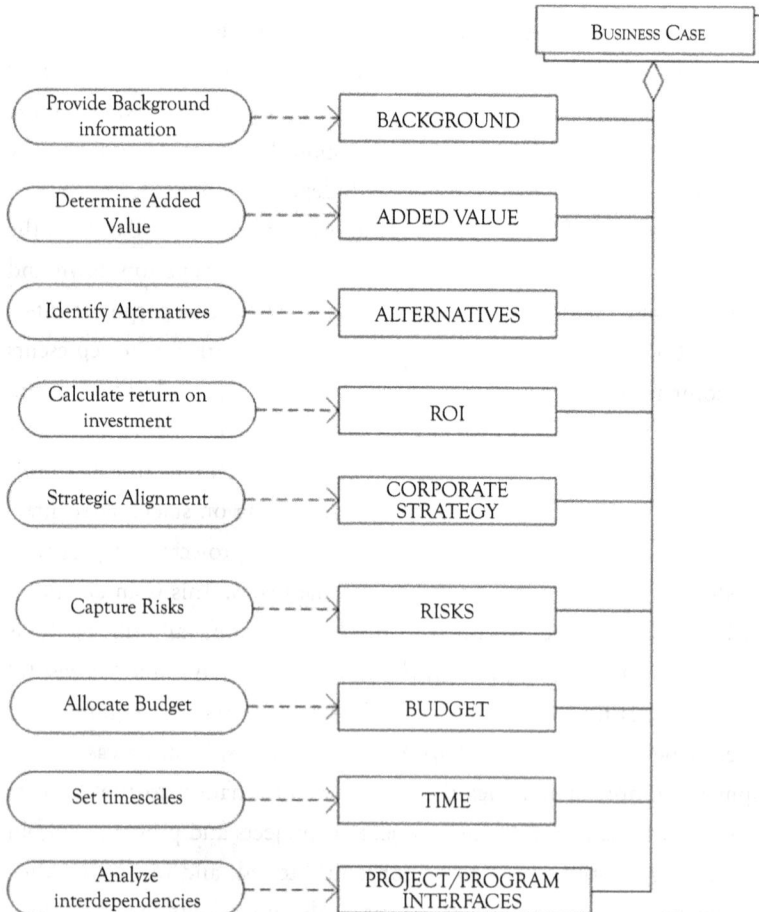

Figure 7.1 Business case development PDD

general idea, including a description of its roots. Every project and program is rooted in an original idea, but it is not an assembly line. Furthermore, a statement on feasibility is required. For business case owners, background information also relates the project or program idea to the organizational core business. This means that the project or program should be aligned with corporate strategy. Background information should address the latter. Following Archibald's (2004) classification of project-based organizations, either the project or program is a means to capitalize on capability (the primary business model of project-driven organizations) or supports other organizational goals (significant to project-dependent organizations).

Determine Added Value

Definition of the added value of the project or program stemming from expected outcomes is paramount for the business case. Without any objectively established, ideally measurable, defined added value, the business case looses its purpose. Added value provides the foundation for benefits management as from the description of added value benefits can be derived. In HybridP3M, it is important to distinguish between outcomes, capabilities, and benefits, an activity of realizing benefits. The quality of the described added value in the business case makes the latter activity easier in the context of the associated process strongly tied with business case development. It should be noted that the added value is not necessarily *direct* financial gain. There are plentiful of nonfinancial motives thinkable that are more of strategic and tactical nature. If, however, the link with economic benefits is poorly established, the corporate budgeting process may become an obstacle.

Identify Alternatives

Alternative in the context of a business case is ambiguous. An alternative may refer to an alternative project or program, competing from the same corporate pool of resources, with different outcomes but similarly, and importantly, aligned with corporate strategy. Or alternative may refer to the current conceptualized project or program with similar outcomes but a different approach. In case of the latter, input from project definition in the form of the project approach is essential. The chosen project approach co-shapes the business case. In identifying alternatives, both types of alternatives should be taken into account.

Calculate Return on Investment

There exists no more objective measure for the financial added value of projects than return on investment (ROI). The major limitation of using ROI, however, is that financial assumptions usually do not hold. Especially in case of complex situations and great uncertainty, the applicability of ROI is a utopia. It is up to corporate management or portfolio management to use this method as a reliable approach for business case evaluation. Hence, tailoring business case development may involve skipping this type of content. Arguably, ROI has more value in predictive situations as compared to agile.

Strategic Alignment

Strategic alignment involves as an activity mapping the project or program with corporate strategy as it is, and at the same time constructing a corporate strategy bottom-up within a framework of current capability (in a proactive manner). As vehicles of change thanks to anticipated and unexpected project outcomes, projects drive corporate strategy fueled by market dynamics and client engagement. A top-down, static strategy simply does not work well for project-based organizations. Therefore, the activity of strategic alignment involves selling projects or programs given the mission, vision, and blue park strategy thanks to eloquent business case development and individual leadership of key project members with decision-making authority.

Capture Risks

It is common knowledge that risks are part of a business case. The reason for this is that risk may jeopardize project outcomes as anticipated or expected. In other words, risk may lead to project failure in basic terms. The risk section of the business case is very dynamic and depends on feeds from risk management. How risks are embedded and described in a formal business case document, however, depends on corporate requirements. Risk management data can be very extensive and therefore may need to be compressed, summarized, or modified according to corporate business case needs.

Allocate Budget

The budget allocated for a project or program reflects expected costs related to overall investment. It is an important control mechanism in combination with budget tolerance. Every corporation has some kind of budgeting process interfacing with business case development in the context of starting up a project or later. While project approval is essentially a responsibility of the project board at the end of initiating a project, at least according to PRINCE2, actual approval in line with the budgeting process may be somewhere else in the organization at corporate or portfolio level. Hence, the link between business case development and corporate management is quite strong and evidence of integrated P3M. As stated in the Introduction, projects are never standalone. It should be noted, however, that fixed budgets have limitations in agile projects, that is, projects characterized by agile delivery. The scope in agile projects is simply too dynamic, and therefore, it is difficult to estimate the required investment. In case of predictive environments where budgets are more realistic, budget tolerance plays an important role in evaluating project success.

Set Timescales

Timescales should not be underestimated in the context of the business case. Timescales enable deadlines and a disciplined mindset. Just like budget, timescales are a control mechanism in combination with timescale tolerance. In case of predictive environments, efficiency thinking has positive impact on the time dimension. In case of agile environments, timescales support definition of stages (stage tolerance for allocated time) and help to control iterations based on priority thinking. On time completion of projects and programs is an indicator of success.

Analyze Interdependencies

Interdependencies relevant in the context of business cases relate to a portfolio of projects and programs in which the success of one project or program depends on the success or performance of others. Dependency can be formed over a period of time as in sequential activity or relate to a fixed, particular, actual period of an evolving portfolio with diverse and simultaneous projects and programs. The most obvious interdependencies reside in the fact that available resources depend on overall allocation across a portfolio. As explained in Chapter 2, HybridP3M's matrix approach optimizes resource usage thanks to a matrix project organization, in which one person can be member of multiple projects at the same time. This specific approach alleviates conflicting interdependencies. Other interdependencies depend more on actual project outcomes of other projects, representing a critical chain at a higher level of planning, namely that of the business case. With regard to external interdependencies, winning contracts is often critical. Another example are party obligations established in contracts.

Process Aspects

Figure 7.2 captures the knowledge nature of business case development.

$$\bigcirc\text{-2} \,\, \circledcirc\text{-1} \,\, \bigcirc\text{0} \,\, \bigcirc\text{1} \,\, \bigcirc\text{2}$$

Figure 7.2 Tacit–explicit continuum of business case development

While business case development assumes externalized knowledge captured in a standard format, the assessment of a business case depends on interpretation and tacit understanding. The explicit knowledge mainly serves as a tool in tacit understanding. What makes a good business case is rather a personal observation. Accordingly, a corporate standard helps to ensure consistency and rationalization but clearly has limitations. Gut feeling in the context of business case justification should not be underestimated.

Figure 7.3 captures the manageability of business case development.

⊙ -2   ○ -1   ○ 0   ○ 1   ○ 2

Figure 7.3 Step-by-step process versus skilled activity continuum of business case development

Business case development is the best example of a step-by-step process in the context of project management. While it relies on tacit knowledge, it is not really a skilled activity from a process perspective. Understanding of the business case deliverable enables execution of business case development. However, the latter does not imply quality output or say anything about viability.

Figure 7.4 captures the specialization level of business case development.

○ -2   ⊙ -1   ○ 0   ○ 1   ○ 2

Figure 7.4 Management–specialist continuum of business case development

Business case development is not a specialization. It is part of the project manager's responsibility. The only nuance here is that the financial analyst is responsible for any financial assumptions, including the ROI analysis. Alternatively, the financial analyst from the matrix organization, positioned in a line function, is the one who tests the project manager's financial assumptions.

Figure 7.5 captures IT support in relation to business case development.

⊙ 0   ○ 1   ○ 2   ○ 3   ○ 4

Figure 7.5 Available IT support for business case development

Business case development does not rely on software. It mainly depends on a template according to corporate standards.

Figure 7.6 captures the complexity of business case development.

○ 0   ○ 1   ⊙ 2   ○ 3   ○ 4

Figure 7.6 Task complexity scale of business case development

Business case development is neither very complex nor simple, but it is in the middle. As a template-driven process, it is perfectly clear what is expected. On the other hand, good business cases rely on experience and a wealth of knowledge.

MAIDEO Requirements

Table 7.1 presents MAIDEO requirements related to "business case development."

Table 7.1 MAIDEO requirements related to business case development

Requirement	Level	Dimension
Formal business cases are used for justification of projects and programs	1	Organization and process
Business cases address added value	1	Organization and process
Business cases identify alternatives	2	Organization and process
Business case includes financial assumptions such as return on investment	2	Organization and process
The business case holds information such as budget and time	3	Organization and process
The business case addresses risk	3	Organization and process
The business case addresses strategic alignment	4	Organization and process
The business case covers interdependencies such as project or program interfaces	4	Organization and process
The business case is used as a tool for strategic alignment	5	Organization and process
The business case is used effectively in the context of portfolio management	5	Organization and process

CHAPTER 8

Realizing Benefits

While having a well-developed business case is useful for project or program justification, it is merely a tool for decision making. A process for benefits management is essential too (see Figure 8.1). In HybridP3M, this process, called realizing benefits, takes the right kind of proactive mindset. It is based on the business need of accomplishment, driving specific activity to ensure the success of a business case. After all, having a good business case is no guarantee for success as many things can go wrong. HybridP3M's realizing benefits process interfaces with business case development, leadership, requirements management, planning, and change management (a corporate or P3M interface). It has a unique process flow; makes a clear distinction between outcomes, benefits, and capabilities; and stresses the importance of a proactive mindset. Benefits never come easily and it is easy to miss opportunity. Note in Figure 8.1 that there are two main parallel processes according to the activity flow. Benefits realization is not a new term as benefits realization management, or simply benefits management, has been addressed before. Realizing benefits should not be confused with controlling benefits. Controlling benefits mainly takes place in the context of additional M&C processes (see Chapter 9, section "M&C Benefits").

Identify Early-Stage Benefits

Early in the life cycle, either starting up or initiation phase, the first step of realizing benefits is to "identify early-stage benefits," which is used as input in business case development in the context of updating the business case. While capture of benefits is also inherent to business case development, the different context determines which roles are engaged, and they differ for these two distinct processes as established in Chapter 2, in

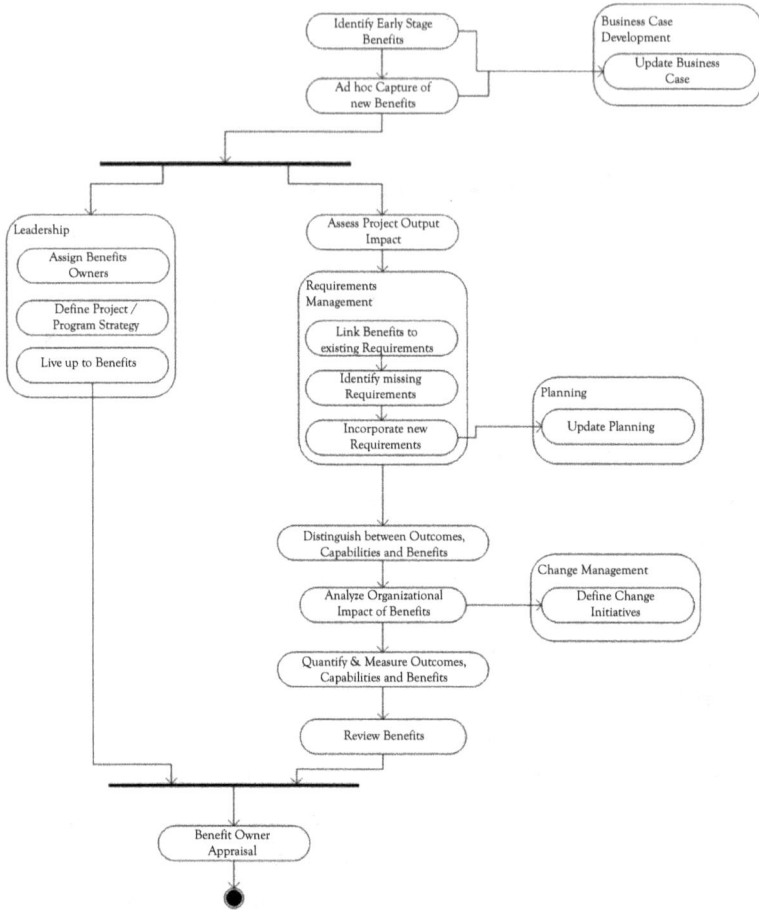

Figure 8.1 Realizing benefits PDD

Matrix 1 (see section "Matrix 1: HybridP3M Processes and Roles"). The identified early-stage benefits are maintained in the business case, which is added to the project brief in starting up a project in the form of an outline and to the project initiation documentation in complete form, in most cases as an attachment to the Project Initiation Document (a single container document). So early-stage benefits play a key role in project and program authorization. Of no less importance, they create incentives based on a common belief that anticipated project and program outcomes are worthwhile, and thereby also foster commitment, a critical project success factor.

Ad Hoc Capture of New Benefits

Whereas the former activity is strongly tied to life cycle, ad hoc capture of new benefits is a continuous process that follows. This activity makes sense because potential benefits can always be identified at a later stage, when new information becomes available or one simply becomes aware of them. Also, as projects and programs unfold, they may develop new organizational capabilities along the way. Such capabilities may result in new opportunity, if spotted, either potential benefits in the context of the current undertaking or at portfolio and corporate level. These "new" benefits should always be added to the business case. This activity is highly important. While business case development is continuous, its purpose is limited, to facilitate decision making and comply with financial systems if present. The activity of benefits identification is much more profound than that. Only with proper understanding of project or program benefits higher level of management can position undertakings and reflect on alignment with corporate strategy, which is arguably a key principle of portfolio management.

Assign Benefit Owners

HybridP3M prescribes the assignment of benefits owners. Benefit owner is not a new concept but often not applied in a project management context. A benefit owner is held responsible and/or accountable for the delivery of one or more benefits through direct project or program involvement or governance from a higher level. The interesting part of a benefit owner is that it transcends the project or program context. It is literally a P3M role with corporate links. That said, the actual benefits owners in a project not necessarily have to be project members like project board members. But in practice, one can expect that in most cases benefits owners are project board members who are responsible for the business case (as representatives of the business case owner). This depends on the makeup of the project board. In PRINCE2, these representatives coincide with the role of executive, but this is only one interpretation of the project board and roles involved. In any case, the assignment of benefits owners is a P3M decision made by higher authorities than project management team or project board members, namely corporate or portfolio management. Additional proof that projects is not a standalone phenomenon. Assigning benefits owners is an act of leadership and therefore depicted in a leadership context in Figure 8.1.

Define Project/Program Strategy

Defining the project/program strategy is also a leadership activity. Depending on the group of benefits owners, this activity is performed either by a project board member who is a benefit(s) owner (and thus an important corporate representative), or project manager on behalf of a corporate benefit owner. The project or program strategy should always be aligned with a corporate strategy, which per definition limits corporate interest in specific capabilities that might be the outcome of new initiatives. Accordingly, corporate strategy favors specific types of benefits associated with certain capabilities. Note that corporate strategy, written or articulated, may cover elements such as drivers and "visionary purpose" according to the mission and vision of an organization (Franken 2016). Regardless of who captures the project/program strategy, both project manager and project board members need to be informed of corporate strategy for the sake of better business alignment and more effective leadership. The project or program strategy is a complex product affected by a usually complex corporate environment, often situated in complex markets. It is hardly standardized information and requires analysis of corporate assumptions of the business, which set preconditions for new initiatives, and are often tacit in nature and biased. This type of reflection of the corporate level may trigger P3M tension in which project members can become critical of corporate assumptions. The latter is significant due to the strategic importance of projects and programs, and thus, the overall position of project managers and project board members. Organizational culture eventually determines how project members will deal with the situation as presented to them, bearing in mind their stake in project success and career prospects. In any case, the project/program strategy combined with effective leadership has a great impact on projects/programs and thus benefits realization across the portfolio. With regard to the contents, the project/program strategy holds various assumptions that determine desired outcomes (which can be vaguely written), providing the foundations for capabilities (corresponding anticipated project results as defined by, for example, features), and affect the management environment or project approach, and so on.

Live Up to Benefits

Live up to benefits is a mindset that drives project behavior with value adding activities directly or indirectly related to benefits. This kind of mindset is essential for the right commitment to results. The best managers are those who focus on project outcomes and who look beyond the delivery of a solution or product (Rosinski 2019). Successful delivery such as the development of a system does not equate project success. For project or program success, benefits realization is essential. And benefits realization is about benefits, not simply capability development. Also capabilities are no guarantee for success. Live up to benefits is a leadership process with success, failure, or something in between as outcome for each specific benefit identified and monitored and controlled. One recommended value adding activity is to define project objectives and to manage people accordingly (e.g., through assignment of small tasks on top the earlier agreed planning). Another value adding activity is to rethink the process model, based on HybridP3M, in terms of practical implementation (the adoption process) taking into account benefits and ideal outcomes. It could be that overall success strongly depends on a particular set of benefits, calling for prioritization. Prioritization of benefits, in turn, may affect functions and processes, or stress the importance of certain work packages and their delivery. The possible process implications of benefits prioritization, established in the process of translating theoretical foundations into practical application, are either scaling processes (based on affordable changes in the spirit of the larger methodology), or investing in processes through the acquisition of knowledge (from possible external sources) and/or tools. It should be stressed that project or program success often depends on commercialization of new products or capabilities, and thus successful marketing. Therefore, there is a limit to benefits realization in the context of projects or programs, and it does not end with their life cycles.

Assess Project Output Impact

The activity of "assess project output impact" follows ad hoc capture of benefits. It is the start of a parallel process next to leadership-oriented activity discussed in the previous sections. And it is followed by requirements management that is triggered by benefits realization. When new benefits are identified, it is important to realize the impact on the delivery process, the anticipated results, or simply project output. When the output needs to be adjusted, the project outcomes need to be redefined. The outcome of "assess project output impact" is a new understanding of the Project Product Description, a PRINCE2 product, or equivalent for intangible project results (linked to change initiatives). It is important that this understanding is recorded as it may lead to significant project change, affecting all levels of the project. If the project outcomes indeed need to be adjusted, then a change control procedure needs to be triggered.

Link Benefits to Existing Requirements

For every captured benefit, the project manager checks whether planned features and related requirements deliver the capability required to support its realization (of the benefit). This involves a study of captured requirements in the context of the next activity: "Link benefits to existing requirements." The underlying assumption is that a study of features lacks necessary detail as successful benefits realization depends on tiny things that can make a difference. Linking benefits, early stage and newly captured, to existing requirements is important in the context of aligning delivery (usually the end product or anticipated capability) with project outcomes, and thus indirectly with benefits, which are the result of actual project outcomes. But more on the intricate relationship between benefits, capabilities, and outcomes is discussed in a later section. It should be noted that a study of requirements by the project manager is not redundant work. It provides an importunity for the project manager to get involved with requirements management in the right context, namely higher level benefits management.

Identify Missing Requirements

Link benefits to existing requirements is followed up by the activity of "identify missing requirements." Whether identified early stage or later in an ad hoc fashion, a benefit that is not supported at a requirement level, or even feature level, is difficult to realize. Therefore, the role of the project manager is to identify missing requirements and present his or her findings to the business analyst. From the discussion that should follow, conclusions should be drawn and new agreement established on new requirements in the delivery process. This may drastically alter the course of a project calling for change in management tactics as the project will be in need of new planning.

Incorporate New Requirements

New requirements arising from the need for end product development or capability building aligned with desired benefits need to be incorporated into the project. This activity, the next step after the gap analysis of the previous activity, involves iterative planning and Agile Product Delivery. It may also involve change management procedure depending on the impact of new requirements (think of affected interdependencies). Once there is a clear picture of the impact of new requirements, the project manager can proceed with updating the planning, and depending on the project organization, will inform team managers on updated work packages. It should be noted that timely identification of new requirements affects optimization of increments and iterations characteristic of agile delivery, a responsibility of Planners supported by Team Managers and feedback from Lead Specialists.

Distinguish Between Outcomes, Capabilities, and Benefits

Once the requirements management activities are completed, the next activity in the flow is to "distinguish between outcomes, capabilities, and benefits." Generally, there is much confusion using all three terms. Then you also have project objectives, used in project definition deliverables.

HybridP3M has not adopted definitions for these terms as they are a bit ambiguous. Instead, HybridP3M makes the following distinction. Outcomes are just like project output results. The difference between outcomes and output is that output is characterized by deliverables or an end product, whereas the outcomes correspond to a changed state, in general. In other words, output is generally tangible, and outcome not necessarily so. So, for example, change initiatives focus on outcomes only, although usually supported by artifacts. Anticipated outcomes need to be identified first in order to define project objectives. The former directs the latter. Capabilities are enablers of added value in terms of strategy, IT, people, and skills, but particularly of operational excellence and products or services. Capabilities are internally or externally oriented and determine which markets are interesting for corporate business. Capabilities can be desired outcomes that relate to a business case (e.g., penetration of a specific market thanks to new capability) or identified as enablers of business outcomes that normally follow new capability (anticipating). Sometimes capabilities depend on the right mix of features and requirements in case of new product development. Capabilities eventually may lead to benefits, as determined by business contracts or reflected by realized value in the internal organization or external environment. For successful businesses, capabilities are characterized by unique selling points and differentiators. The activity to "distinguish between outcomes, capabilities, and benefits" should trigger evaluation of project documentation for consistency of the discussed terminology and foster discussion of benefits. There are various types and levels of benefits depending on the business context and project/program objectives. To develop a simple taxonomy might be beneficial. Examples of high-level, strategic benefits are efficiency savings, improved customer satisfaction, and improved staff satisfaction (Department of Finance 2020).

Analyze Organizational Impact of Benefits

Definition of desired project outcomes enabled by capabilities, and subsequently, project objectives, may lead to capture of strategic benefits. Alternatively, strategic benefits are sometimes derived from corporate strategy, often rooted or disguised as corporate goals or targets, leading to new initiative and formation of projects and programs. In either case, strategic benefits have a big impact on organizations and rather apply to a portfolio of projects and programs instead of individual initiatives. This means that in case of their discovery portfolio management should be triggered, a P3M interface, and in turn other enterprise functions such as marketing (known for supporting benefits realization at the corporate level). On many occasions, successful realization of strategic benefits depends on more than one initiative and various factors, that is , a combination of factors. Awareness of interdependencies in this context calls for commitment on a greater scale than individual projects and programs. This in turn enables projects and programs to trigger complementary change initiatives, which subsequently can be orchestrated at the portfolio level.

Quantify and Measure Outcomes, Capabilities, and Benefits

Once a proper understanding is established of lists of outcomes, capabilities, and benefits, possibly supplemented with a diagram that captures their intricate relationships as in a mapping, the next step is to quantify them so that they can be effectively measured. Usually, outcomes and capabilities are measured at the end of a project or program. Benefits, on the other hand, are usually measured at the end of a project or program but also, and importantly, after official project or program closure since realization of benefits is often a long-term process. However, measurement also may take place during a project or program, especially when duration is long. Measurement of benefits, specifically, also relates to monitoring and control addressed in the corresponding process chapter (Chapter 9) and will be discussed in more depth. It is key that quantitative data is collected. Analysis of such data helps to gain better insight in project or program success. And using metrics to this end is arguably an objective way to develop such insights. It is also key that outcomes and benefits in particular are quantifiable in the first place and described accordingly.

Review Benefits

The activity of "review benefits" follows contemplation of benefits realization and the outcome of the previous activity, namely measurement of benefits. Following the assumptions in the previous section, the review process may take place during, at the end, or after a project or program. It depends on realistic timescales of benefits realization as compared to the duration of the project or program itself. In case of a postmortem review, sometimes long after the end of project or program, review activities are planned based on a Benefits Review Plan, an official PRINCE2 product. The review process itself is key in the understanding of project and program success (explaining performance of project teams), and success in relation to corporate goals at a more strategic level. When the designated time for realization of specific benefits has elapsed, review findings should be passed on to portfolio management for historical record and as information that can be used for future reference.

Benefit Owner Appraisal

HybridP3M prescribes the activity of "benefit owner appraisal" for every benefit owner by an organizational member occupied with this HR task. This activity takes place at the right time, taking into account the time aspect of benefits, and in the right setting (aligned with human resource management policies). The goal of benefit owner appraisal is to increase commitment levels to benefits. Good performance should be rewarded, and bad performance should at least provide lessons learned. Benefits realization without benefit owner appraisal does not reinforce the proactive mindset advocated at the beginning of this chapter. So it is an essential activity.

Process Aspects

Figure 8.2 captures the knowledge nature of realizing benefits.

$$\bigcirc -2 \quad \bigcirc -1 \quad \bigcirc 0 \quad \bigcirc 1 \quad \circledcirc 2$$

Figure 8.2 Tacit–explicit continuum of realizing benefits

Benefits management according to HybridP3M relies on explicit knowledge related to benefits or externalization of tacit knowledge. Such explicit knowledge is key in creating a transparent process in which benefits can be quantified and measured.

Figure 8.3 captures the manageability of realizing benefits.

○ -2 ○ -1 ○ 0 ○ 1 ◉ 2

Figure 8.3 Step-by-step process versus skilled activity continuum of realizing benefits

There is no simple activity flow with regard to realizing benefits. Related activity is triggered when the time is right in alignment with business pressure. This requires a proactive attitude and significant experience. Realizing benefits and taking ownership of benefits in the process are a skilled activity enabled by profound understanding of benefits management, and it is not a step-by-step process in terms of procedure.

Figure 8.4 captures the specialization level of realizing benefits.

◉ -2 ○ -1 ○ 0 ○ 1 ○ 2

Figure 8.4 Management–specialist continuum of realizing benefits

Benefits (realization) management is not a specialization; it is management work mainly performed by project managers, while benefits owners are held responsible and accountable for actual outcomes. So this process requires generic management skills.

Figure 8.5 captures IT support in relation to realizing benefits.

◉ 0 ○ 1 ○ 2 ○ 3 ○ 4

Figure 8.5 Available IT support for realizing benefits

There hardly exists software in support of benefits management. Traditionally, benefits data can be managed in deliverables. Yet there is a commercial package that claims to support benefits management automation, called Wovex (https://wovex.com).

Figure 8.6 captures the complexity of realizing benefits.

○ 0 ○ 1 ◉ 2 ○ 3 ○ 4

Figure 8.6 Task complexity scale of realizing benefits

Realizing benefits is a complex process, interfacing with leadership, requirements management, planning, and change management. Related activity needs to be planned taking into account life cycle dynamics and potential work triggers.

MAIDEO Requirements

Table 8.1 presents MAIDEO requirements related to "realizing benefits."

Table 8.1 **MAIDEO** *requirements related to realizing benefits*

Requirement	Level	Dimension
Senior management identifies realizing benefits as distinct process that complements business case development	1	Strategy and policy
Realizing benefits interfaces with business case development based on interdependencies	1	Organization and process
Realizing benefits interfaces requirements management linking benefits with requirements	2	Organization and process
Realizing benefits assigns benefits owners	2	Organization and process
Benefits play a pivotal role in the development of a project or program strategy	3	Strategy and policy
Benefits owners live up to benefits, a just qualification of their mindsets	3	People and culture
Outcomes, capabilities, and benefits are properly distinguished	4	Organization and process
Benefits are quantified so that they can be measured	4	Monitoring and control
Benefits are reviewed when the time is right	5	Organization and process
Benefits owners are appraised based on their leadership, including commitment to benefits	5	People and culture

CHAPTER 9

Monitoring and Control

Monitoring and control (M&C) is a HybridP3M process derived from the enterprise function bearing the same name (see Figure 9.1). As a function and enterprise dimension, M&C has an old tradition rooted in efficiency thinking. In the context of project-based organizations, M&C traditionally focused on control of project anomaly based on planning deliverables. This was in the time when waterfall thinking was dominant and delivery predictive. In the current era, in which agile methods changed the project management landscape, the purpose of M&C needs to be reconsidered as project planning strongly depends on the delivery model and as a reaction to shorter planning horizons, a trend that started with agile delivery. Observation shows that agile methods collectively fail to address the project management implications of M&C, similar to support of other essential project management functions like planning. It is not without a reason that HybridP3M, like many other experts, stresses that agile approaches are not project management methodologies. They are simply not comprehensive enough, either too implicit or lacking guidance entirely. And as compared to any available method in the realm of project management, HybridP3M takes the quality of being a holistic body of knowledge to a whole new level, thanks to the combination of functional achievement and P3M interfaces in particular, but also coverage of the topic of leadership, principles, and so on. Taking all of this into account, HybridP3M has expanded the scope of the M&C process to address benefits, planning (becoming less dominant), delivery (to ensure productivity, quality, and safeguard agility), stakeholder commitment, and change (promoting change management and a controlled change procedure). Every activity in this process is the responsibility of the controller, a distinct, complementary project role that needs to be promoted in today's business (just like the project knowledge manager).

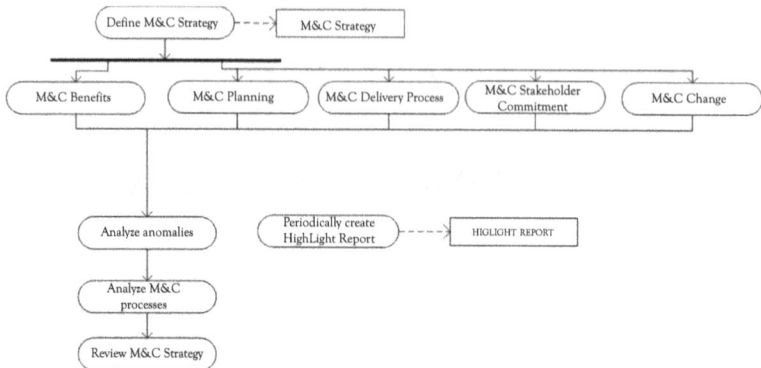

Figure 9.1 *M&C PDD*

Define M&C Strategy

According to Wim Scheper, basing his insight on work of Merchant and Van Der Stede (2003), there are essentially three forms of control, namely result control, people control, and action control, which may complement each other. Result control is performance based. It is the type of control set by targets (enabled by systems that measure performance) and maintained by incentives (e.g., reward for performance). A characteristic of result control is that organizational members enjoy a large degree of individual freedom. The focus is on meeting targets, not how they are met. The pitfall of result control is to not address gamesmanship, which contradicts fair play. People control is culture based. Every organization uses people control, aware of it or not. People control is primarily formed by socialization processes, rooted in value-driven behavior (or lack of values in amoral cases) and cultural expression in general. A key management mechanism for people control is the recruitment process in combination with a recruitment policy, for attracting the "right" people. Another mechanism are training concepts. Action control limits the freedom of individuals by limiting their actions or enforcing certain actions based on various control systems (sometimes IT based). Monitoring of behavior is a dominant theme in action control. A useful metaphor for action control is looking over one's shoulder.

The three main forms of control should provide the foundation for the M&C strategy of a project or program, the output of the first M&C activity (as depicted in Figure 9.1). In this strategy deliverable, as formal capture is preferred over informal communication, it is explained how each form of control applies to the project or program in question. Usually, the strategy depends on corporate policy and systems, so tailoring an approach is limited and possibly directed top-down (a potential P3M interface).

M&C Benefits

After definition of the M&C strategy early in a project's or program's life cycle, various parallel processes of M&C unfold. One of them addresses the area of benefits. M&C of benefits complements the realizing benefits process and review of benefits activity in particular, and it is not considered as redundant. It is namely performed by the controller, an extra responsibility complementing the work of the project manager, project board, financial specialist, and corporate management, who deal with benefits management according to realizing benefits. The controller monitors benefits by monitoring enabling capabilities that rely on project outcomes, but also conditions (market or organization wise) affecting the latter outcomes or long-term benefit realization. Since benefits need to be managed *during* a project or program, enabling steering (and thus a degree of agility), this often requires foresight and prediction of outcomes. Conditions, on the other hand, are always actual but may change, and thus any change needs to be anticipated. Based on his or her analysis, the controller may conclude that benefits are under threat. If that is the case, he or she needs to alert the project manager who will trigger the activity of "review benefits," a process interface escalating the issue in the context of realizing benefits. So the controller himself or herself does not take any further control measures.

M&C Planning

A traditional interpretation of project success in terms of project performance is delivery on time, on budget, and on scope. These three aspects also correspond to the three variables of the triple constraints model (a well-known PM concept): time, cost, and scope, in which manipulation of one variable affects the other two and quality in the middle. While the triple constraint model reflects the interdependencies logically, it is not a useful management tool as decision making regarding time, budget, and scope is not a simple process, and not a project manager's task. It is an oversimplification of stakeholder decision rationale. That said, the three variables are embedded in planning and need to be measured, for example, against baselines in case of predictive delivery. Measurement of these project level variables enables a record of performance useful for project evaluation and establishment of project success. Much more common than performance measurement in this context of M&C is the adjustment of planning, also for the sake of having up-to-date schedules, essential to progress tracking and task coordination. In case of predictive delivery (only), performance measurement and schedule information are sometimes combined to gain advanced insight as follows from earned value management (EVM). EVM is a technique for the measurement of performance based on objective analysis of progress. The three key metrics of EVM are actual costs, planned value, and earned value. Actual cost is the budget that has been consumed up to a specific point in time. Planned value is the amount of allocated budget for a specific point in time according to original planning. And earned value is the amount of work that has been completed in reference to the original project budget. Generally, one can say that EVM is a rather rigid approach and strongly relies on accurate baselines. In dynamic, uncertain environments, demanding an agile approach, EVM is never an option.

M&C Delivery Process

The controller role is also responsible for M&C of the delivery process. This responsibility complements the role of the team manager with regard to delivery. While the team manager leads a team of specialists and mainly supervises work, the controller holds a record of actual working hours and cost related to specific tasks actually performed. He or she uses this data for updating actual schedules (used for coordination purposes) and the "project history plan" (for evaluation purposes), consolidated based on the former. So the controller has a better picture of performance in terms of numbers and should report or discuss progress with the team manager. The controller should also pay attention to control of quality by examining whether completed work satisfies quality requirements or explicit or implicit quality standards. It is either the controller or team manager who is responsible for updating the Quality Log (or Register), a PRINCE2 product and activity. Generally, the team manager is more concerned with day-to-day business, directing team members and making sure things are getting done. The controller, on the other hand, observes delivery more from a distance and lacks authority to direct team members, such as the assignment of work. This unique position of the controller enables him or her to make observations from a tactical point of view. In particular, the controller should monitor how agile the overall delivery process is practiced and communicate his or her findings to the team manager. Agility will depend on the incremental and iterative character of delivery and on satisfaction of customer requirements, taking into account priority levels.

M&C Stakeholder Commitment

Stakeholder commitment depends on effective stakeholder management, including the popular notion of stakeholder engagement. However, commitment can only be influenced to a certain degree. It is also a function of stakeholder interests and focus, which in a dynamic world, just like attention, shifts. So managers should be aware of another potential mystique: overestimating the effect of stakeholder management. That said, stakeholder commitment is a critical success factor and therefore needs to be monitored. As commitment is difficult to measure by traditional means of data collection (except some clever use of survey), it needs to be observed and assessed informally. Therefore, the controller role needs to be present during key meetings and discussions between the project board and the project manager. Additionally, the controller should study made decisions and the decision-making process behind them. The controller also needs to have a conception of commitment and understanding of cultural differences and various attitudes. A key indicator of commitment is arguably buy-in. Buy-in refers to the degree stakeholders support the overall business case based on their stake in the project or program, sometimes a separate business case (in case of a commercial customer/supplier environment). But there are many more possible indicators. Examples are devotion to the adopted process model, application of project assurance (as part of project direction), cooperation with the business analyst for requirements gathering, feedback on new system releases, public relations via corporate media channels (promoting the project/program), quality control indicating interest in project output, and so on.

M&C Change

The final parallel M&C activity relates to change. Change may apply to (desired) project outcomes, project output (the deliverables, end product) depending on requirements and actual results (irreversible or not), the management environment (e.g., modification of a process), benefits, contractual agreement with third parties, the project organization (and resource management), project or program assumptions, regulation, risk, and other areas. The controller should monitor change based on observation, enquiry, and data collection (in particular the output of the change control procedure). In his or her analysis, the controller should do a couple of checks. First of all, determine whether the change affects the business case, in either a positive or negative way. Second, the controller should check whether the change affects planning. Third, the controller should check whether the change affects the process model as part of the management environment. Other checks are imaginable. Based on the findings, the controller should report to the project manager and provide feedback on the data collected thanks to application of the change control procedure. It should be stressed that the change control procedure, if properly applied, enables a consistent, coordinated approach to change management. And a double check by the controller certainly helps to (1) better map the impact of change and (2) validate responsive measures and taken decisions.

Analyze Anomalies

The parallel M&C activities described above enable responsive management of expectations. In any management environment, there exist expectations. These expectations combined may well provide the justification of a project or program. Thanks to M&C, one can determine whether expectations are realistic, need to be adjusted, or corrective actions are needed to keep the same expectations maintained as realistic. In other words, M&C relies on data collection and control measures in order to anticipate expectations. Expectations in all key control areas are essential in developing understanding of any specific project and program. Accordingly, as fundamental assumptions, expectations minimize uncertainty based on understanding. Having expectations provides key project members an important frame of reference for using management principles, the type of management characterized by control and exception management.

Unexpected project behavior, which often can be traced back to people's actions or wrong assumptions in the first place, may result in project anomalies in one or more of key control areas. While M&C should initiate corrective measures, the complexity of an anomaly may demand closer examination, in retrospect (more specifically, at a later reflection moment during a life cycle), for effective resolution, understanding, or learning purposes. In contrast, "immediate anomaly resolution" (based on any means of control) is simply part of M&C. Hence, the activity of "analyze project anomalies," performed by the controller, follows an initial M&C response to an anomaly. When M&C of an anomaly initially proves ineffective, this may provide the foundation for the development of a case (problem+solution scenario) and iterative decision making (Rosinski, 2019). Here, we are dealing with "contemplated anomaly resolution" or "rationalization of anomaly." So the notion of potential iterations complicates the activity flow of M&C. The activity of "analyze project anomalies" requires additional time and resources for reflection and an opportunity to reflect, such as Gate reviews.

Analyze M&C Processes

M&C mainly relies on data collection, data analysis, and observation. It makes sense to implement systems and IT tools that generate insights from data and collect data in the first place. Digital transformation applied to projects and programs, or project analytics, may play a large part in this respect, although it is still in its infancy. Second, it makes sense to learn from project anomalies as to better anticipate project outcomes and behaviors in the future. As project anomalies may explain project failure, it is critical to understand them thoroughly in terms of cause and effect. Lessons Learned may reveal that M&C activities were ineffective or inappropriate and lead to follow on recommendations for process improvement.

Review M&C Strategy

The final M&C activity in the activity flow is "review the M&C strategy." In the context of this activity, the controller reflects on the M&C strategy adopted in the beginning. It takes place at the very end of a project, when all Lessons Learned are reviewed (tested for validity), aggregated, and consolidated. The review should consider all three types of management control (recall that these are result control, people control, and action control), how they were embedded into the project or program, and whether changes are required according to new understanding or Lessons Learned with Follow-On Action Recommendations.

Periodically Create Highlight Report

The final activity addressed by M&C, which is independent from the depicted activity flow in Figure 9.1, is to periodically create a highlight report. This activity, which is triggered mainly by time, is adopted from the PRINCE2 methodology. In PRINCE2, the highlight report serves to keep project board members informed of progress (with traditional planning deliverables as the main baselines). In HybridP3M, this purpose is extended to inform all stakeholders and corporate leaders (with a particular interest in the project or program) on progress and other relevant information, tailored to satisfy information requirements.

Process Aspects

Figure 9.2 captures the manageability of M&C.

$$\bigcirc\text{-2} \quad \bigcirc\text{-1} \quad \circledcirc\text{ 0} \quad \bigcirc\text{ 1} \quad \bigcirc\text{ 2}$$

Figure 9.2 Tacit–explicit continuum of M&C

M&C relies on a combination of tacit and explicit knowledge. There is no predominance of one type.

Figure 9.3 captures the manageability of M&C.

○ -2 ○ -1 ○ 0 ○ 1 ◉ 2

Figure 9.3 Step-by-step process versus skilled activity continuum of M&C

M&C is a skilled activity, and it is not a step-by-step process. It takes experience to learn M&C methods and techniques and to apply them in the right context. Therefore, a distinct controller role should be part of the management team.

Figure 9.4 captures the specialization level of M&C.

○ -2 ○ -1 ◉ 0 ○ 1 ○ 2

Figure 9.4 Management–specialist continuum of M&C

M&C is neither a typical project management responsibility nor specialization. It is somewhere in the middle. So the project manager can evolve into a proficient controller.

Figure 9.5 captures IT support in relation to M&C.

○ 0 ○ 1 ◉ 2 ○ 3 ○ 4

Figure 9.5 Available IT support for M&C

M&C according to HybridP3M's interpretation is a diverse process. There is no software on the market that deals with all of its aspects. But there are tools that support specific niche areas. For example, work flow software is a form of action control.

Figure 9.6 captures the complexity of M&C.

○ 0 ○ 1 ○ 2 ○ 3 ◉ 4

Figure 9.6 Task complexity scale of M&C

M&C is a complex process considering all the aspects involved. M&C involves a number of key parallel processes consisting of complex activity. This complex activity is difficult to organize according to a step-by-step process. Rather, M&C relies on best practices (applied in the right situation or context).

MAIDEO Requirements

Table 9.1 presents MAIDEO requirements related to "monitoring and control."

Table 9.1 MAIDEO requirements related to M&C

Requirement	Level	Dimension
There is a M&C process complementing planning, using baselines as a tool	1	Organization and process
There is a M&C process for the delivery process	1	Organization and process
M&C initiates corrective measures	2	M&C
There is an explicit strategy for M&C at the corporate level	2	Strategy and policy
There is an explicit strategy for M&C at the project or program level	2	Strategy and policy
The explicit strategy for M&C takes into account all three forms of control, including result control, people control, and action control	3	M&C
There is a process for M&C of benefits	3	Organization and process
There is a M&C process for change	4	Organization and process
The M&C strategy at the project or program level is reviewed based on new, ongoing developments	4	Organization and process
There is a M&C process for stakeholder commitment	5	Organization and process
Corrective measures are based on thorough analysis of anomalies	5	Organization and process
The M&C strategy at the corporate level is periodically reviewed	5	Strategy and policy

CHAPTER 10

Managing Stakeholder Expectations

While sometimes addressed in best practice literature, stakeholder management is an area that often lacks process support in practice (see Figure 10.1). In practice, project managers often have to rely on their own experience and personal understanding of stakeholder needs. And the available literature on this topic did not result in standardization. While everyone acknowledges the importance of stakeholder management, people often have different interpretations of it as a process. At the extreme, one interpretation is that managing stakeholders is an oxymoron, that stakeholders cannot be managed. In less extreme form, this means that stakeholders shape the management environment and cannot be influenced easily, which is a reasonable presumption. Arguably, it depends on the ability to communicate with senior officials (often representing the key stakeholders) and leadership. HybridP3M only can offer process guidance as an additional asset and acknowledges that there is a limit to the extent of being able to influence stakeholder positions. Note that influence is a better word choice than manage. Furthermore, HybridP3M has adopted the popular notion of stakeholder engagement. The overall process could be seen as a proactive approach to managing stakeholder expectations, which according to HybridP3M, in principle, can be managed. The guiding forces of this process are responsiveness, satisfaction (in terms of benefits, information requirements), and learning. Learning is key because due to inexperience or misunderstanding big mistakes are often made in this context. The project manager is responsible for managing stakeholder expectations, with very limited support by project support, in some administrative areas.

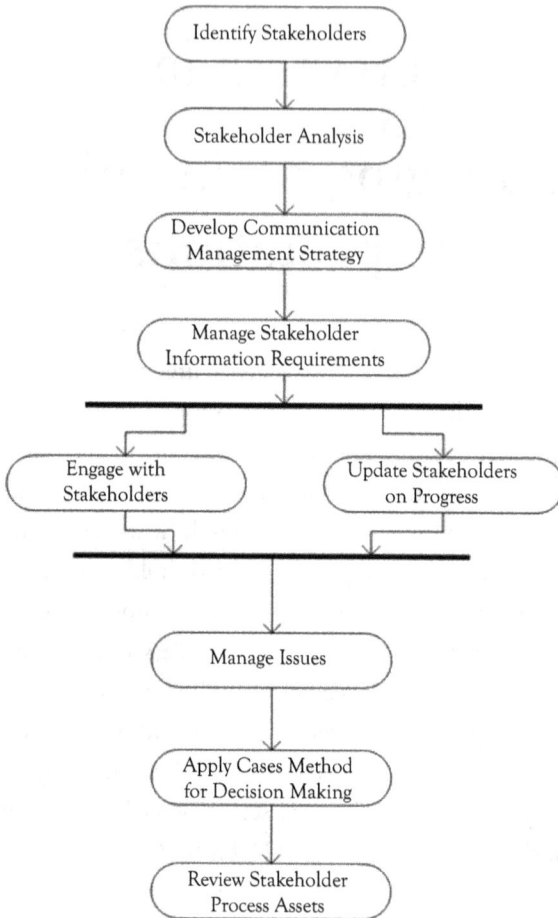

Figure 10.1 Managing stakeholder expectations PDD

Identify Stakeholders

Early in the project and program lifecycle, the first step related to stakeholder management is to identify the stakeholders. There are two groups: (1) stakeholders with authority or decision-making capability and (2) stakeholders without a decision-making role but with interest in overall success or success in a particular area that addresses their specific needs. The first group includes project directors. For example, PRINCE2 identified three main stakeholders belonging to this group as part of the project board: the executive (representing the business case owner), senior supplier, and senior user. In practice, the composition of the project board may be more complex and include various project sponsors or unique business case owners, depending on the type of commercial customer/supplier environment. The second group may include various project supporters with a stake or basic interest (people in relation networks who support the greater cause of the undertaking and specific reasons behind it, with or without deep political motives), external consultants, external institutions (with a shared political or commercial interest), and users who are not represented on the project board, not even in the name of the senior user. Note that project supporters, active on social media, for example, can affect project outcomes; they are stakeholders by no mistake.

Stakeholder Analysis

The second step that logically follows is stakeholder analysis. The goal of stakeholder analysis is to develop an understanding of the people who represent stakeholders, rather than something abstract, and the analysis should definitely avoid inappropriate generalizations (due to false fantasies or projection on people with a certain organizational background—read stereotypes). The implication of this approach is that it is paramount to get to know people who they really are and better understand their background, their position in strategical terms based on their unique interest in the undertaking, and accordingly their drives or motives. Hence, stakeholder analysis relies on communication, a people skill, and observation, an analytical skill. Therefore, it is not some kind of mapping that you put on paper, rather it is a process of engagement and learning. The tacit dimension of stakeholder analysis should not be underestimated. The outcome of stakeholder analysis includes a better understanding of stakeholder needs, stakeholder expectations, and stakeholder information requirements. The latter two aspects can be managed according to a sound process.

Develop a Communication Management Strategy

Following stakeholder analysis, the next step is to develop the communication management strategy. This activity and corresponding product are adopted from the PRINCE2 method, which generally fails short of stakeholder management as it provides no distinct process nor subtheme (this observation accounts to all editions, up to the sixth one). The communication management strategy is a formal document that uses the outcomes of stakeholder analysis, in particular (but not limited to) stakeholder information requirements, to define a communication strategy for each stakeholder who needs to be updated on progress. Communication management theory is highly beneficial as input here, for insight and validation of communication assumptions. The strategy is not merely meant to create conditions for effective and efficient satisfaction of information or knowledge needs; it also serves as a means to manipulate the general picture on certain project or program aspects, to the benefit of the project organization or parts of it, in the interest of overall success for each or specific major business case involved. In conclusion, this activity consolidates findings from stakeholder analysis, puts them into a nice report, and results in a document that provides the foundation for correspondence and communication, formally and less formally.

Manage Stakeholder Information Requirements

Armed with a communication management strategy, defined early in a project's or program's life cycle, the project manager should have a clear view of stakeholder information requirements, at least early stage, enabling more focused communication efforts. However, the needs of stakeholders are dynamic as projects and programs unfold and are sometimes unexpected therefore. So there is a need to manage stakeholder information requirements as they arise, anytime, during the project. In other words, upfront capture and subsequently establishment of stakeholder information needs—for coordinated communication efforts—have limitations here. The activity to manage stakeholder information requirements advocated here does not imply a formal procedure, just awareness of the importance of ad hoc information provision and knowledge needs satisfaction. With the right attitude in communication combined with the communication management strategy, which partly explains what and how to communicate, the project manager is ready to engage meaningfully with stakeholders, in alignment with any applicable corporate policies adopted, according to the former strategy. Ultimately, the effectiveness of communication (taking into account specific objectives) will depend on social skill (such as responsiveness) and knowledge of communication management as a science, but the presence of a communication strategy certainly helps. In practice, sometimes it is as simple as to follow up on enquiry. The daily log, a PRINCE2 concept, effectively should play a role in the capture of ad hoc information needs, as this is often critical information.

Engage with Stakeholders

Following management of stakeholder information requirements, resulting in their capture and internalization, a process unfolds of two parallel activities: the activity to engage with stakeholders and the activity to update stakeholders on progress (a specific form of engagement with a clear goal), both which rely on satisfaction of information requirements. Stakeholder engagement has two main aspects: information processing and relationship development. The former can be approached from an analytical perspective and thus is a rational process in principle. The latter, however, has important social dimensions, making it very complicated. The countless of social factors include goodwill, shared understanding (also an information processing problem), shared values, to identify with one another, lines of authority, and organizational structure in general. HybridP3M believes that the primary purpose of stakeholder engagement is to create social conditions that enable sound decision making, as transparent as needed depending on the political environment. Sound decision making here implies making rational choices taking into account alternatives and various other criteria relevant to the decision-making process as professionally conceived by the decision makers or expected by those affected (sometimes considered by authority figures in the light of transparency). In terms of relationship development, it suffices to create understanding and develop trust. Liking each other or similar is not the main theme here. This means that stakeholder engagement does not have to be fun. It should be above all functional. Accordingly, HybridP3M does not suggest creative social interventions, nor provide socialization guidance. But the social factors mentioned earlier make relationship development difficult and complicated.

Update Stakeholders on Progress

Progress information relates to key information requirements, popularized in project management literature. For example, PRINCE2 has dedicated a whole theme to progress. These information requirements are so important because they are essential for decision making, including go and no-go decisions in the stage-gate model, depending on the receiver of the information. One mechanism to update stakeholders on progress is the highlight report, created in the context of monitoring and control (see Chapter 9). The exact contents of this highlight report will depend on situational characteristics and the targeted stakeholders. In any case, the contents should not be limited to technical aspects, such as brief summaries of activity duration and completion dates (derived from planning data). This is where stakeholder management complements the narrow vision of monitoring and control and optimizes sharing of information in terms of relevance and quality. But even with flexible contents, the highlight report is just one of the possible means to update stakeholders on progress. Other formats and methods may apply in this context as well. Another approach worthwhile of mention are progress dashboards inherent to software solutions. Their main disadvantage is that they are tools and thus require user acceptance, either a major challenge (of software adoption) or not feasible at all. Moreover, there is no standardization of progress information to this date, and thus no consensus on the desired data, making current software solutions fallible. A better alternative, arguably, is social methods of correspondence and use of social media. Note that social media is key to inform more distant stakeholders (e.g., project supporters and community members) and stakeholders who are sensitive to public relations on formal channels or via personal networks.

Manage Issues

Issue management is a common theme in project management. HybridP3M has adopted the PRINCE2 activity of "capture and examine issues and risks" and the follow-up activity of escalating issues and risks (which is triggered if necessary), in the context of the Agile Delivery subprocess of monitoring and control at the project level (see Chapter 16). In this delivery context, the focus is on progress, a narrow view often limited to management-by-exception. It does not address all problems at the level of stakeholders. Therefore, HybridP3M has included the activity of "manage issues" in the context of stakeholder management. Issues that relate to stakeholders should always be top priority of the project manager and project board. The profound impact of such issues should never be underestimated. The implications of stakeholder level issues can endanger the whole project, posing risk at the very least. These implications may (1) change the management environment drastically, compromising Hybrid-P3M's principle of a stable management environment, (2) negatively affect management processes (compromise the adopted process model), (3) complicate delivery (due to a change in acceptance criteria), or (4) even lead to a premature end of the undertaking or plain project failure, provided that resolution is not an option or has failed. If however resolution is an option and decision making applies, for the best possible outcomes and consensus, the next activity of "Apply Cases method for decision making" becomes relevant to issue management and could be considered a subprocess. However, decision making is not limited to resolution of issues, and thus, the latter activity is adopted as an extra subprocess (follow-up activity) of managing stakeholder expectations (see the next section).

Apply Cases Method for Decision Making

Decision making in projects and programs is an important theme according to HybridP3M. Decisions are constantly made on various levels and involve different actors based on the context of the decision made or to be made. As HybridP3M strongly believes in joint process responsibility, decision making in HybridP3M projects and programs is often characterized by deliberation (defined as long and careful consideration by key actors), which depends on analysis, dialogue, discussion, and if a time period applies reflection as well. Sometimes stakeholders are involved in decision making, other times not. But all strategic and some tactical decisions may affect stakeholders, and therefore, depending on the impact, the position of stakeholders should be taken into account. HybridP3M sees wrong decision making as one of the greatest or most frequent causes of project failure. Therefore, HybridP3M suggests that the decision-making process should be supported by the Cases method introduced by ProwLO (Rosinski 2019). The Cases method is a management tool that can be applied in an iterative fashion. It is based on the general assumption that problems can be resolved in one or more iterations depending on the outcomes (i.e., project behaviors) of taken decisions and actions. The Cases method has a dual purpose: problem solving during a project and learning across projects (e.g., enabling Case-based reasoning). For what the Cases method exactly entails and how it precisely works, please refer to Rosinski

(2019). The benefits of using a formal approach like the Cases method as to guide decision making and reflect on the decision-making process include making rational choices (as bounded as they may be), consideration of stakeholder interests, and valuable data accumulation for project assurance (as decision making is an interesting area for the project assurance function, holding decision makers accountable for their choices).

Review Stakeholder Process Assets

There is a lot of potential data to be collected about stakeholder management, and a lot can be learned from experience. Accumulation of stakeholder knowledge is highly valuable, also in the context of learning across projects and programs. For example, stakeholder analysis can be useful in future projects and programs when engaging with the same stakeholders again. The accumulated stakeholder knowledge, in turn, may transform stakeholder management processes targeted at unique stakeholders. Essentially, these processes of communication, use of social media, and decision making depend on stakeholder and stakeholder management knowledge, combined with HybridP3M's methodological knowledge. This type of process development could result in the creation of various process knowledge artifacts, ideally maintained in a knowledge base. One process area of significance is the education of particular stakeholders in stakeholder management according to HybridP3M, in particular HybridP3M's unique approach to decision making and the use of the Cases method in this respect. HybridP3M takes decision making to the next level, and most stakeholders will appreciate this unless there are political motives in play (contradicting a culture of openness).

Process Aspects

Figure 10.2 captures the knowledge nature of managing stakeholder expectations.

Figure 10.2 *Tacit–explicit continuum of managing stakeholder expectations*

Stakeholder management is originally the domain of tacit knowledge. While managing stakeholder expectation does lead to externalization of tacit knowledge, effective stakeholder management mainly depends on tacit assumptions, not always captured or communicated. Without a formal process for stakeholder management, most knowledge would remain tacit. The exchange of stakeholder information would also be limited to socialization processes.

Figure 10.3 captures the manageability of managing stakeholder expectations.

$$\bigcirc \text{-2} \;\; \circledcirc \text{-1} \;\; \bigcirc \text{0} \;\; \bigcirc \text{1} \;\; \bigcirc \text{2}$$

Figure 10.3 Step-by-step process versus skilled activity continuum of managing stakeholder expectations

Managing stakeholder expectations according to HybridP3M's definition is a step-by-step process rather than skilled activity. Hence, it can be managed and promoted effectively based on corporate standards. The activity flow is rather straightforward although work triggers need to be established carefully in alignment with planning and life cycle dynamics.

Figure 10.4 captures the specialization level of managing stakeholder expectations.

$$\circledcirc \text{-2} \;\; \bigcirc \text{-1} \;\; \bigcirc \text{0} \;\; \bigcirc \text{1} \;\; \bigcirc \text{2}$$

Figure 10.4 Management–specialist continuum of managing stakeholder expectations

Stakeholder management is not a specialization. It should be performed by generalists.

Figure 10.5 captures IT support in relation to managing stakeholder expectations.

Currently the market does not specifically support stakeholder management. As a process, stakeholder management is simply not well established. Existing CRM software is not useful here. On the other hand, the question is whether the process requires software tools in the first place. Stakeholder management could be considered a manual process based on human skills not in need of automation.

Figure 10.6 captures the complexity of managing stakeholder expectations.

$$\circledcirc 0 \quad \bigcirc 1 \quad \bigcirc 2 \quad \bigcirc 3 \quad \bigcirc 4$$

Figuare 10.5 Available IT support for managing stakeholder expectations

Stakeholder management is a complex process just like most social activity. For example, it takes time and skill to understand and establish the needs of stakeholders.

$$\bigcirc 0 \quad \bigcirc 1 \quad \bigcirc 2 \quad \circledcirc 3 \quad \bigcirc 4$$

Figure 10.6 Task complexity scale of managing stakeholder expectations

MAIDEO Requirements

Table 10.1 presents MAIDEO requirements related to "managing stakeholder expectations."

Table 10.1 MAIDEO requirements related to managing stakeholder expectations

Requirement	Level	Dimension
Stakeholder analysis is a standard procedure in projects and programs	1	Organization and process
All stakeholders are identified at the beginning of the project or program	1	Organization and process
Stakeholders are updated on progress at the right time and in the right place	2	Monitoring and control
There is a proactive approach to managing stakeholder expectations	2	People and culture
The project or program defines a communication management strategy or equivalent	3	Organization and process
Stakeholder engagement plays a key role in relationship building with stakeholders	3	People and culture
Stakeholder information requirements are managed proactively	4	Organization and process
Issues related to stakeholders are managed professionally	4	Organization and process
The Cases method is applied in the context of decision making relevant to issue management	5	Organization and process
Stakeholder process assets are reviewed at the end of the project or program	5	Organization and process

CHAPTER 11

Managing Requirements

Requirements management is the work of the business analyst, who essentially acts as a link between the customer and the project management team with regard to solution development. As a process, requirements management or managing requirements is well documented and relatively mature (see Figure 11.1). This can be evidenced for example by the numerous tools that exist to support this process. In most cases, these tools focus on software engineering. An example of a popular feature is history tracking based on the notion of "requirements traceability," often associated with requirements management. In practice, the business analyst has a direct communication link with the customer or key user representative (e.g., senior user), but in case of meetings is often accompanied by the project manager, who is responsible for supporting requirements management as proactively as possible. It should be stressed that the business analyst is the main actor, not the other way around. The approach in HybridP3M is characterized by make-or-buy decisions, depending on knowledge gaps, and the user experience (UX) plan. UX is a relatively new paradigm based on the fact that users have increasingly demanding expectations with regard to friendliness, aesthetics, functionality, simplicity, and purpose of solutions. The UX plan utilizes knowledge to develop a better view of such expectations and may refer to existing literature on topics like usability and provides a useful frame of reference in the context of requirements gathering. In case of software engineering, there exist many front-end (design) software development frameworks that specifically address the needs of users in the light of UX, sometimes combined with more technical requirements. An example is the front-end framework Bootstrap. The antithesis of requirements management is that system design is a work of art, to be liked or not by users.

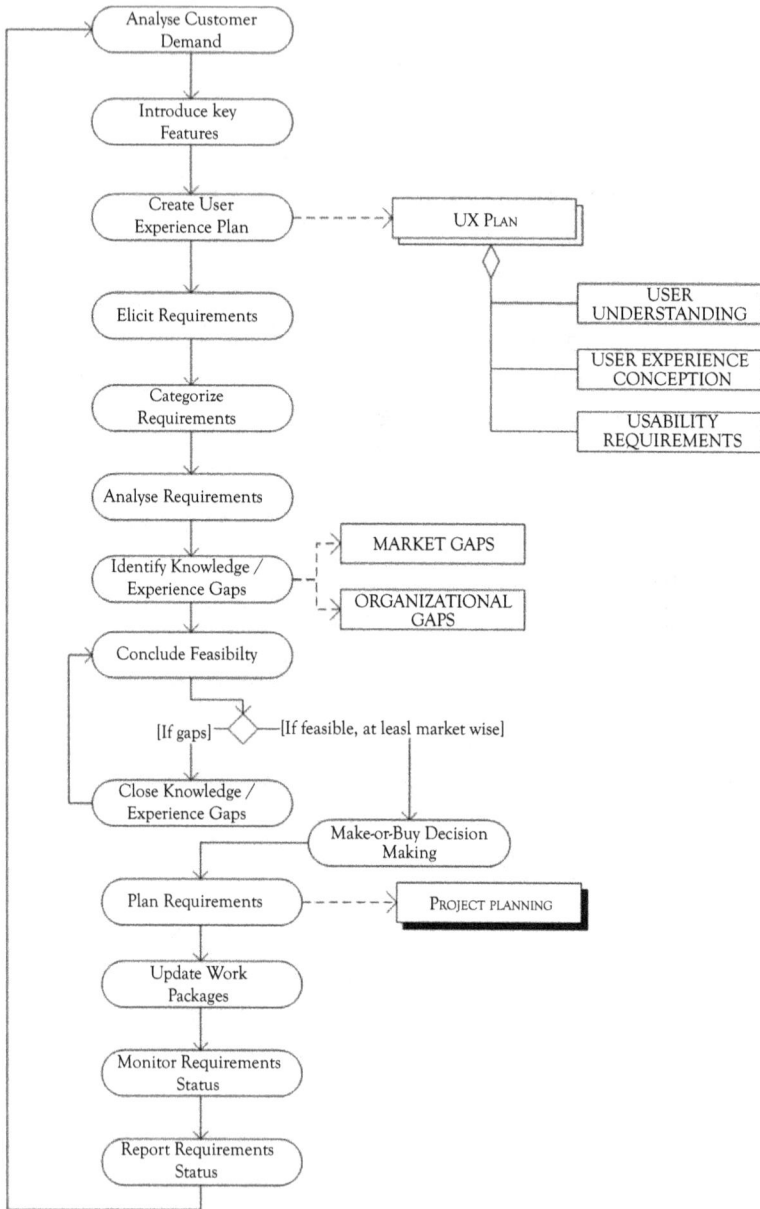

Figure 11.1 Requirements management PDD

Analyzing Customer Demand

The first step in managing requirements is to analyze customer demand. This activity is performed at the beginning of the life cycle but is subject to change due to the dynamic character of projects. In case of (complex) uncertain projects, which prefer agile approaches (read Agile delivery models), customer demand is not an easy given in the beginning of an undertaking. In such cases the step to analyze customer demand is rather a continuous process, triggered on multiple occasions over time, depending on changes and change governance. In any case, an initial understanding of customer demand is essential for the project or program (which is obvious as it is part of the foundation of an undertaking). The project manager should have the same level of involvement as the business analyst in the context of this first step. Essentially, the team should apply interviewing techniques and optionally rely on previous stakeholder knowledge, accumulated over time. Similar projects with the same stakeholders may repeat over time. The concept of customer relates to a customer/supplier environment, commercial or in-house organized. The latter relates to a customer and supplier in the same organization but different departments. For example, the IT department may be responsible for the delivery of system to be used by a different department within the same organization. The customer is essentially the party who profits from a unique business case and introduces the solution to a group of users, another potential third party and, thus, is a key stakeholder. The customer is always represented on the project board. Sometimes the business analyst is in contact with the senior user role, other times with someone who acts like an executive, either way someone who has a conception of what needs to be delivered. However, the business analyst should take into account all potential user groups of the solution. Interfacing with stakeholder management, the business analyst should assess their expectations as well. So while the customer is a key sponsor of the project or program, demand may not apply to a singular body only, depending on stakeholder analysis. Hence, input of other stakeholders could be valuable in this process of understanding (customer) demand.

Introducing Key Features

The second step, after analyzing customer demand, is to introduce key features. Features represent a modular approach to functionality, in which each feature has one or more functions. System design is well known for functional analysis. Features are rather high-level functions as there are multiple levels of functions. Alternatively, features can be interpreted or replaced by qualities, also applicable to less tangible project outcomes. A quality is simply a characteristic or attribute defined by quality criteria. Other classifications of features are not essential. Most important is the notion that there are multiple levels and types of requirements, corresponding to specific features.

Creating User Experience Plan

Once a set of key features has been established the next step is to create the UX plan. This plan consists of three parts: (1) user understanding, (2) UX conception, and (3) usability requirements. Based on user understanding, it is possible to define user or stakeholder profiles (based on assumptions, generalizations). User profiles, in turn, help to make predictions about user behavior, such as human–computer interaction or specific utilization of new assets in general. Such predictions have an impact on design and other requirements. They enable alignment of user expectations and actual supply based on anticipation (based on generalized knowledge), modification (driven by adjustment), and prioritization (according to a hierarchy of user needs). It should be noted that not all requirements are established by the customer. Some are provided by the supplier, who has a historical, general understanding of the customer based on market knowledge. Likewise, some requirements are historical, others are innovative. This activity, to create a UX plan, highly relies on knowledge reuse, generally. So managing requirements is an interesting interplay between the various parties and different roles involved. The second part, UX conception, combines the supplier's conception of UX with the customer user's conception of UX. This involves externalization of supplier's knowledge of UX and enquiry of customer user's interpretation of UX. This combination should result in some level of alignment or reconciliation. The third and final part is a list of usability requirements. This list is generated based on accumulated knowledge (across projects) on the topic of usability and updated thanks to customer feedback. Usability requirements correspond to design choices that relate to usability or quality standards. It should be noted that usability plays a central role in

UX. Usability as a science, which predates UX, is popularized by Jakob Nielsen (see e.g., Nielsen 1993). An example of a usability requirement in web development is the ability to sign up on new platform via existing accounts of other, more established platforms (like Gmail or LinkedIn) using application programming interfaces (APIs).

Eliciting Requirements

"Eliciting requirements" relates to "requirements gathering" (rather proactive acquisition), requirements discovery (unplanned or ad hoc), and requirements capture (externalization, articulation), and depends on the iterative nature of delivery. It is a key responsibility of the business analyst. This activity is considered by some as very important because the captured requirements provide the foundation for the project's architecture as part of the end result (i.e., end product or intangible counterpart). As mentioned in a previous section, the origins of requirements are potentially diverse. As put by BA-Experts (YouTube 2016), eliciting requirements is not a trivial task. While different roles may, contribute to eliciting requirements, it is the business analyst who must ensure their input is taken into account, timely, and adequate, and consolidate the results in a document that can be used by other processes or in a later phase of requirements management (such as planning requirements). The activity of eliciting requirements is arguably a tacit skill (e.g., inherent to interviewing) but also relies on knowledge reuse of explicit knowledge.

Categorizing Requirements

"Categorizing requirements" should follow elicitation. There exist many classification schemes for requirements, which can be found on the internet. The business analyst should adopt one or tailor one according to corporate or project needs (a corporate standard is recommended). HybridP3M does not favor one specific approach over another; it depends on the situation. A common divide is the distinction between functional and nonfunctional requirements. Another example is performance requirements. Also, categorization may depend on the use of a specific software tool (enforcing a particular scheme). The benefit of categorizing requirements is that it provides contextual information and a means to organize information. Requirements are sometimes also referred to as specifications, a term often used in relation to customer demand.

Analyzing Requirements

Once requirements are categorized and classified, the next activity is to analyze them. The outcome of analysis is a better understanding of the expected solution to be developed. More specifically, analysis helps to define or redefine scope after analysis of customer demand. An important aspect of analysis is to check the architecture, which is shaped by requirements, for integrity. Architecture integrity mainly depends on consistency of requirements and potential conflict due to conflicting requirements. Architectural integrity should not be confused with feasibility, which will be discussed later. Analysis also implies mapping of organizational capability necessary to support incorporation of requirements. Understanding of necessary capabilities in this specific context is the first step in establishing knowledge/experience gaps, the follow-up activity discussed next.

Identifying Knowledge/Experience Gaps

"Identifying knowledge/experience gaps" is an extension of the previous activity, analysis of requirements. Gaps reveal potential inability to meet requirements. Such inability, in turn, may compromise the conceptualized solution, often against the will of the customer or users. Resolution of this problem is to either accept off-specifications beforehand (and agreed with the customer) or as outcome of delivery processes or, alternatively (and ideally), solve the problem by closing the gap. Gaps are a key factor in determining the feasibility of the solution based on specific requirements, but they are not the only one (e.g., organizational resources also play a role). To conclude, feasibility is the next step that follows. But first it is key to identify knowledge/experience gaps at the organizational level (not just project level as there exist methods of knowledge transfer). Next, closer examination of gaps at the organizational level may reveal that there are gaps at the market level as well, a real risk. In order to identify knowledge/experience gaps at the organizational level, it is essential to know what an organization knows and compare that information with what is required. So this activity relies on research or access to knowledge about the organization, including its capabilities, skill base, and people (as carrier of knowledge or host of experience).

Concluding Feasibility

After identification of organizational or market knowledge/experience gaps, relevant in the context of specific requirements, the next step is to conclude feasibility. There are two potential outcomes here: (1) there are gaps at any level that make part of the anticipated solution not feasible or (2) the solution is feasible, either from the viewpoint of the supplier organization or market-wise. In case there are gaps this calls for resolution. There are different scenarios possible for resolution. In case there is a gap at the project level but not at the organizational level, there is an opportunity to close the gap. In practice, however, the latter depends on effective knowledge transfers or opportunity for learning and training (when skills are the focus point). A more drastic intervention is a change in team membership directed from above (corporate resource management). If there is a project level gap and organizational level gap at the same time, but not a market level gap, then the market should play a role, *potentially* influencing make-or-buy decisions or the decision to hire external expertise (in the light of "integrated management," in which a high level of control is exercised over third parties provided specific interdependencies). So organizational gaps essentially imply knowledge development or knowledge acquisition. If there is a project level gap that can be explained by a market level gap, then knowledge development is called pioneering work.

Closing Knowledge/Experience Gaps

Once feasibility has been concluded and the conclusion is partly rooted in knowledge/experience gaps that can be solved, then the business analyst should trigger efforts to close these gaps. This calls for a systematic approach and proper knowledge management. Therefore, the business analyst provides a letter of recommendation to the project knowledge manager who takes this activity to the next level. The project knowledge manager oversees knowledge processes critical in the process of closing the gaps through management interventions, that is to say, definition and coordination of activities supporting knowledge processes such as knowledge transfer, knowledge development, and knowledge integration. The project knowledge manager works closely with the project manager in order to get the required authorizations and certain level of support necessary for any planned knowledge management activities. Activities planned in the context of inter-project learning or communities-of-practice call for support from other actors (key formal and informal authority figures) as well. After the performance of knowledge management interventions the activity to conclude feasibility is invoked again.

Make-or-Buy Decision Making

Once feasibility has been concluded and the conclusion is that the solution is feasible, at least market-wise, then make-or-buy decisions are made. Make-or-buy decisions have been scientifically researched and there exist theories that make predictions (or at least have explanatory capability) such as "Transaction Cost Theory" and "Resource-Based View." These theories are certainly interesting and recommended for reading, but in practice, according to HybridP3M, decision making is a process that is hardly influenced by theoretical assumptions. Instead, it is assumed that decision making reflects anticipation to unique events, calling for unique approaches, or similar events (across projects), which may benefit from case-based reasoning (applied to the domain of management). In fact, most decision makers will lack this level of education in the first place and, thus, are most likely unaware of the scientific foundations/ramifications underlying their role in decision making and the decision-making process. Much more important is to gain experience in decision making and learn from past successes and failures. A general assumption in make-or-buy decisions, adopted by HybridP3M, is that the decision to buy is more likely when there is an organizational knowledge/experience gap that can be filled by the market, that is to say, a third party able to satisfy specific requirements. It should be stressed that make-or-buy decisions are prepared by the business analyst and performed (executed) by project manager, possibly in a joint fashion with multiple decision makers or project board members.

Planning Requirements

The activity to "Plan Requirements" follows make-or-buy decisions. This activity is an example of "integration management," a past knowledge area in the old *PMBoK* manuals. Planning interfaces with actual delivery. So planning requirements affects delivery. And the chosen delivery model affects requirements management in terms of incremental, iterative thinking. In case of Agile delivery, planning requirements takes into account the iterative nature of projects and programs. In case of predictive delivery, planning requirements is mainly upfront activity.

Updating Work Package

In the context of stages, following lifecycle dynamics, the activity of planning requirements results in updating the Work Packages. In HybridP3M, Work Packages have either a direct or an indirect relationship with requirements. In case of an indirect relationship, Work Packages follow Stories, a popular Agile notion. Stories do imply specific requirements to be met, however. The use of Work Packages is inherent to Agile product delivery according to HybridP3M (see Chapter 16).

Monitoring Requirements Status

Successful requirements management depends on tracking requirement status. Monitoring requirement status can be automated using software tools. But such an approach requires consistent and organization-wide use of an IT tool, a great challenge. Therefore, monitoring requirements manually, although a bit outdated, is not a silly idea. The administrative burdens can be reduced by focusing on high-priority requirements.

Reporting Requirements Status

The final activity introduced in the context of managing requirements is the activity to "report requirements status." Depending on stakeholder requirements, it is good practice to report such information. In the light of process automation and the popularity of dashboards, reporting can be replaced by access to information in secure IT environments, targeting the right stakeholders or members of the project management team.

Process Aspects

Figure 11.2 captures the knowledge nature of managing requirements.

○ -2 ○ -1 ○ 0 ○ 1 ◉ 2

Figure 11.2 Tacit–explicit continuum of managing requirements

Requirements management depends on explicit knowledge. Every-thing relevant in the context of requirements is externalized. Only externalization enables integration of requirements. Ironically, the capture of requirements requires specific skills (like eliciting) with a more tacit dimension.

Figure 11.3 captures the manageability of managing requirements.

○ -2 ◉ -1 ○ 0 ○ 1 ○ 2

Figure 11.3 Step-by-step process versus skilled activity continuum of managing requirements

Requirements management is a step-by-step process. The most diffi-cult are make-or-buy decisions and the closing of knowledge/experience gaps, but they are joint responsibilities.

Figure 11.4 captures the specialization level of managing requirements.

○ -2 ○ -1 ○ 0 ◉ 1 ○ 2

Figure 11.4 Management–specialist continuum of managing requirements

Requirements management is a specialization performed by the business analyst. In practice, however, the business analyst's role is sometimes performed by the project manager.

Figure 11.5 captures IT support in relation to managing requirements.

○ 0 ○ 1 ○ 2 ○ 3 ◉ 4

Figure 11.5 Available IT support for managing requirements

There exist many software tools to support requirements management, mainly in the domain of software development. It is vendor philosophy that effective requirements management requires tracking capability.

Figure 11.6 captures the complexity of managing requirements.

○ 0   ○ 1   ○ 2   ◉ 3   ○ 4

Figure 11.6 Task complexity scale of managing requirements

Requirements management is rather a complex process. The specific activities demand experience and skill. Also the interfaces with planning and delivery make it a complex process.

MAIDEO Requirements

Table 11.1 presents MAIDEO requirements related to "managing requirements."

Table 11.1 MAIDEO requirements related to managing requirements

Requirement	Level	Dimension
Analysis of customer demand is a continuous process.	1	Organization and process
Key features or desired qualities provide the foundation for specific requirements.	1	Organization and process
Advanced methods or techniques are applied to elicit requirements.	2	Organization and process
Requirements are categorized consistently across projects or programs.	2	Organization and process
Requirements are properly analyzed.	2	Organization and process
Requirements analysis leads to identification of knowledge or experience gaps.	3	Organization and process
Feasibility analysis is tied to requirements.	3	Organization and process
Conclusions on feasibility are used as an argument in make-or-buy decisions.	3	Organization and process
Conclusions on feasibility trigger activities directed at closing knowledge/experience gaps.	4	Organization and process
Requirements are reported to the right people at the right time and in the right place.	4	Monitoring and control
The organization uses requirements management software with monitoring capability.	4	IT
Make-or-buy decisions are a joint responsibility.	5	People and culture
Requirements are integrated efficiently in the context of integration management.	5	Organization and process

CHAPTER 12

Evaluating the Project or Program

Project evaluation is an opportunity not only for project management but also for project knowledge management (PKM). This chapter focuses on the former, contributing to the project management perspective of evaluating projects/programs. The PKM perspective is elaborated in the context of ProwLO, based on a separate guidance (Rosinski 2019). HybridP3M considers project evaluation, the final frontier of project management, not, for example, benefits management. The reason is multifold. It is undervalued, unpopular, and therefore not well developed. HybridP3M aims to change this situation. Second, building on the first reason, one can observe that due to lack of experience (as a result of missing practical application), involved actors are not provided with the opportunity to learn the skills involved, nor the opportunity to develop the right attitudes considering the political dimension of evaluation. To some extent evaluation remains a mystery. Third and finally, following the first reason, without a proper understanding of project evaluation, the current status quo, learning across projects remains elusive. Project evaluation is essential in the context of realizing learning organizations, and thus, optimization, a key HybridP3M objective. Schindler and Eppler (2003) once noticed that there are distinct process and content aspects to project evaluation methods. HybridP3M recognizes that the evaluation process from an activity perspective is subject to details and sensitive to best practices. Accordingly, this acknowledgment may motivate development of corporate formats for project evaluation, tailored according to corporate needs and scalable according to specific project needs. Inspired by Schindler and Eppler, HybridP3M has introduced a meta-level process to adopt evaluation methods, based on unique corporate formats. Second, HybridP3M has defined standard content elements to be derived from evaluation. These elements imply activity for their capture. However, HybridP3M allows flexibility depending

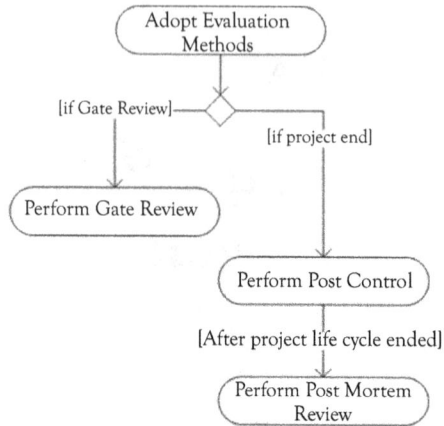

Figure 12.1 *Meta-process of evaluating projects/programs*

on the selected evaluation method and context of evaluation, such as the moment during a lifecycle. In order words, HybridP3M permits to some degree tailoring. Figure 12.1 depicts the meta-process of evaluating projects/programs, whereas Figure 12.2 focuses on evaluation method essentials, content-wise.

Adopting Evaluation Methods

At the beginning of the life cycle, a decision needs to be made on what kind of evaluation methods will be used in the project or program. This decision involves the particular formats available and the relevant associated timing. Developing corporate formats, aligned with Hybrid-P3M's guidance, is basically a common knowledge need. According to HybridP3M, there are three different formats at the fundamental level: (1) gate reviews, which benefit from the stage-gate paradigm, (2) post control (at the end of the lifecycle), and (3) postmortem reviews (at some future point after project closure). It is important that this decision takes place at the beginning because evaluation, taking up time and resources, needs to be planned in advance for mutual agreement. Evaluation in an ad hoc fashion is simply a too chaotic approach.

Performing Gate Review

Gate reviews are very important. One of the benefits is that gate reviews provide a reflection opportunity on decision making. Decision and taken

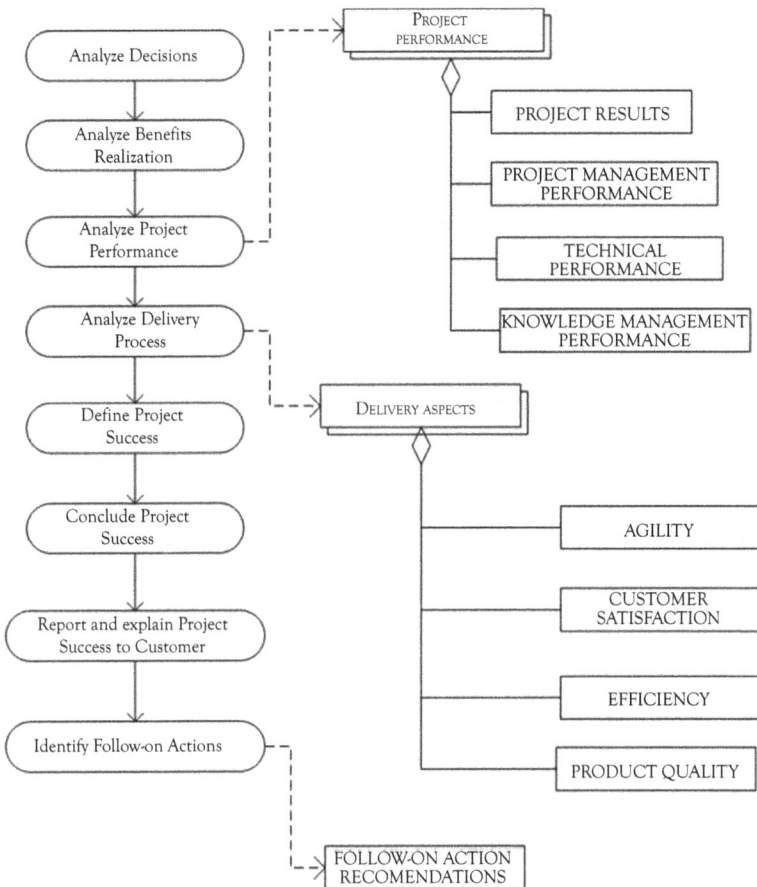

Figure 12.2 Evaluation method essentials

actions take time to take effect. Changes in project behavior can only be noticed thanks to the right amount of time elapse. When decisions are made regarding the next stage, there is an opportunity to reflect on project behavior of the ending stage or earlier stages. This allows corrective measures such as to revoke earlier made decisions or making new decisions to deal with existing problems or new problems as they may evolve. In other words, gate reviews are a perfect tool for iterative decision making, supported by the Cases method.

Performing Post Control

Post control complements gate reviews and provides an opportunity for consolidation of newly gained knowledge rooted in experience. Post control as a method was originally introduced by Schindler and Eppler, and they compared it to other approaches like project audit, after action review, and post-project appraisal. In HybridP3M, post control depends on the selected format for project/program evaluation. From an output perspective, however, it is recommended to adopt HybridP3M's content suggestion. In practice, the extent of evaluation is always a function of the strategic importance of a project or program and also depends on the business pressure to move on to the next project.

Performing Postmortem Review

Postmortem reviews complement post control mainly in terms of evaluating benefits as benefits realization takes time in most cases. Also after the project or program has ended, there may be better time frame to organize evaluation and hold a moment to reflect. The main problem with postmortem reviews, and to a lesser extent post control, is that project amnesia becomes significant. People simply tend to forget, and personal experiences, including a view on historical events, do not always reflect facts.

Analyzing Decisions

The first major element of project evaluation is analysis of decisions. The goal here is not to create a culture of blaming; instead a culture of openness is advocated. But even a culture of openness, if any organization claims one, has its limits due to present authority relations, decision power, confidentiality, and politics. These factors contribute to the condition that team members respect decisions as they are keeping an "appropriate" distance to the decision-making authorities, at the cost of potentially constructive criticism. But if an organization deeply wants to learn, then decision makers should take accountability for their actions and allow a health check. There are two approaches possible, or a combination. Analysis is restricted to introspection for the benefit of individual learning, or analysis takes place in the context of group learning, including dialogue and discussion, and gets reported for the benefit of systematic organizational learning. The advantage of the first approach is the greater respect for confidentiality. The advantage of the second approach is knowledge validation and greater knowledge integration of captured results.

Analyzing Benefits Realization

The second major element of project evaluation is analysis of benefits realization. This type of analysis involves a reflection on the business case. The most relevant question in this context is whether it was a good investment. How good an investment it was really depends on actual benefits realized. As mentioned earlier, it may take time to identify or measure actual benefits. In some cases, benefits will be recurring thanks to exploitation of new capability. Some benefits might be monetary, others of a more strategic nature. Every type of benefit needs to be taken into account based on the adopted benefits management approach.

Analyzing Project Performance

Organizations that take professionalization of project and program management seriously need to analyze project performance systematically. Project performance is a complex concept consisting of four elements: project results (deliverables and outcomes), project management performance (taking into account variables such as time and cost), technical performance (specialist work), and knowledge management performance (e.g., alignment with corporate-level KM strategy), which are no simple concepts either. It takes experience and intelligence to develop an appropriate conception of each of these elements, a conception that enables assessment, ideally supported by metrics. HybridP3M has no easy solution for this and recommends organizations to develop this knowledge independently. However, each element can be assessed informally based on tacit knowledge. That would be the initial situation (an immature approach). Another issue is whether this specific analysis is not better performed in the context of an audit by project external people (e.g., external consultants or internal members of quality assurance). The benefit of the latter approach is increased objectivity and specialization in all relevant aspects. But HybridP3M believes that a project audit can complement but not replace personal evaluation of project performance by the key actors involved. It is namely a part of growing and learning by individuals.

Analyzing Delivery Process

Analysis of the delivery process is arguably an easier activity, partly thanks to the fact that the project management team may rely on customer feedback. It is not confined to an evaluation of internal performance, subject to personal views based on personal stakes. Again intelligent use of metrics can make this activity more objective. It should be stressed that this activity should be performed during the project (in addition to project end, possibly project postmortem) so that things can be adapted based on the lessons learned. Analysis of the delivery process takes into account pure delivery aspects, and there are four identified, namely: (1) agility, (2) customer satisfaction, (3) efficiency, and (4) product quality. The first element requires a common understanding of Agile, possibly supported by a definition. As the customer may benefit from better results thanks to Agile delivery, he or she should express his or her view on the incremental, iterative, and generally flexible character of the delivery process as experienced firsthand (supported by effective change management), or provide main concerns (e.g., raise the fact that the delivery actually lacks/ lacked agility). Assessment of customer satisfaction completely relies on customer feedback. Assessment of efficiency, on the other hand, takes into account cycles of development and requires performance measures. Depending on the industry, the organization should develop its own approach to measuring efficiency. Finally, product quality is a measure partly depending on quality metrics (number of faults, quantified rework, an account of user acceptance, etc.) and partly depending on the subjective perception of the end result by the customer.

Defining Project Success

Project success has no universally accepted definition. In fact, it is a relatively obscure concept. As stated by Rodolfo Siles (2020), "Project success has been historically defined as a project that meets its objectives under budget and under schedule." This definition, perhaps in line with the major bodies of knowledge (competing with HybridP3M), clearly associates performance with success through the latter part of the statement. But HybridP3M views success independent of performance. Analysis of project performance, as described earlier, stands in its own right (and thus the greater good of performance management). So according to HybridP3M, objectively speaking, success refers to the degree to which objectives are met, which are dynamic by the way in an Agile, realistic context. But success also depends on interpretation and a personal view of the greater meaning of a project or program. In such a context, benefits and outcomes are crucial. Project success becomes something real when benefits and outcomes can be quantified and measured; otherwise it is just an opinion. This stresses the importance of benefits management. A popular interpretation of project success is when the project satisfies customer and/or specific stakeholders. But this is only one perspective. Therefore, HybridP3M recommends to develop common understanding of project success, or at least facilitate a healthy discussion, and usage of a definition of success useful in the process of closing the project and final handover, concluding results and opening a serious evaluation opportunity.

Concluding Project Success

At the end of the project, in preparation of final handover, project success must be concluded based on the previously deliberated and accepted definition. Findings on performance, based on analysis of project performance, are of secondary importance but may compensate any harsh conclusions, such as project failure, placing success in a greater perspective. The conclusion should be recorded and shared with the project management team and project board, so a final report can be prepared for the customer.

Reporting and Explaining Project Success to Customer

HybridP3M thinks that it is in the interest of the supplier to communicate the conclusion on project success with the customer. In case there is success, this can only have a positive effect, a reason to celebrate. And in case success is partial or lacking, reasons for why can be explained. Reporting and explaining can only do good in terms of public relations. It is a gentleman's approach. Success is not an end result, thanks to new capability benefits may materialize later and learning may prove invaluable. This should always be taken into account.

Identifying Follow-On Actions

In order to make an impact, evaluation should lead to improvement. In this respect, follow-on actions play a key role. As a conceptual knowledge need, follow-on actions are often derived from cases and lessons learned in the context of knowledge management. But from a project management perspective, the roots of follow-on actions are of secondary importance. Essentially, follow-on actions suggest changes. These changes may apply to operations, but sometimes also relate to tactics or strategy. Thanks to definition of actions the suggested changes have practical meaning. In conclusion, follow-on actions are a highly "actionable" knowledge type. If regarded and taken seriously at the corporate level, they may drive institutionalization of change. The quality of follow-on actions highly depends on the quality of the evaluation process and capture of related knowledge types like cases and lessons learned.

Process Aspects

Figure 12.3 captures the knowledge nature of evaluating the project or program.

$$\bigcirc \text{-2} \quad \bigcirc \text{-1} \quad \bigcirc \text{0} \quad \circledcirc \text{1} \quad \bigcirc \text{2}$$

Figure 12.3 *Tacit–explicit continuum of integrating knowledge management*

In order to become a repeatable process, evaluation should rely on explicit process know-how. The social dimension of evaluation will always maintain the position of tacit knowledge in the process.

Figure 12.4 captures the manageability of evaluating the project or program.

$$\bigcirc \text{-2} \quad \circledcirc \text{-1} \quad \bigcirc \text{0} \quad \bigcirc \text{1} \quad \bigcirc \text{2}$$

Figure 12.4 *Step-by-step process versus skilled activity continuum of evaluating the project or program*

Evaluation is essentially a step-by-step process. Therefore, it can be promoted based on corporate standards effectively. Proficiency, however, depends on skilled activity.

Figure 12.5 captures the specialization level of evaluating the project or program.

$$\bigcirc \text{-2} \; \circledcirc \text{-1} \; \bigcirc \text{0} \; \bigcirc \text{1} \; \bigcirc \text{2}$$

Figure 12.5 Management–specialist continuum of evaluating the project or program

Evaluation is a generic management skill but could be considered a specialization as well. It does not require a distinct role however. Project managers, supported by project knowledge managers, require training to perform evaluation well.

Figure 12.6 captures IT support in relation to evaluating the project or program.

$$\circledcirc \text{0} \; \bigcirc \text{1} \; \bigcirc \text{2} \; \bigcirc \text{3} \; \bigcirc \text{4}$$

Figure 12.6 Available IT support for evaluating the project or program

Evaluation itself does not rely on IT for support. The associated documentation, however, should be integrated based on document management solutions with knowledge integration capability.

Figure 12.7 captures the complexity of evaluating the project or program.

$$\bigcirc \text{0} \; \bigcirc \text{1} \; \bigcirc \text{2} \; \circledcirc \text{3} \; \bigcirc \text{4}$$

Figure 12.7 Task complexity scale of evaluating the project or program

Evaluation is a relatively complex process due to the social setting in which it takes place. Also business pressures and life cycle dynamics pose potential barriers to evaluation.

MAIDEO Requirements

Table 12.1 presents MAIDEO requirements related to "evaluating the project/program."

*Table 12.1 MAIDEO requirements related to evaluating the project/
program*

Requirement	Level	Dimension
Senior management has an explicit policy for project or program evaluation.	1	Strategy and policy
The organization applies some form of post control.	1	Organization and process
The organization applies gate reviews consistently.	2	Organization and process
The organization has developed coherent and holistic evaluation methods and techniques, inspired by existing standards such as HybridP3M.	2	Organization and process
The organization applies project postmortem reviews in order to better evaluate benefits.	3	Organization and process
Various aspects of project performance are evaluated.	3	Organization and process
Various aspects of delivery are evaluated.	3	Organization and process
Project success is defined and evaluated accordingly.	4	Organization and process
Project success as concluded is communicated with the customer and explained.	4	Organization and process
Follow-on actions are defined in the context of evaluation.	5	Organization and process
Follow-on actions are taken seriously by corporate management or portfolio management.	5	People and culture
Key decisions are analyzed including the unique decision-making process behind them.	5	Organization and process

CHAPTER 13

Leading the Project or Program

Leadership in the context of an organizational setting is a popular theme both online and offline (see Figure 13.1). On various media, leadership discussions tend to propagate a certain leadership style as righteous as opposed to other styles. What is regarded as righteous depends to a large extent on human values. Sometimes a distinction is made between leadership and management in which the two are contrasted (Zaleznik 1993). Whatever the perspective, leadership touches various traditions of management, including Taylorianism and anti-Taylorianism. In any case, it is a popular discussion and an interesting field for study. In the context of HybridP3M, leadership is a tool to build a successful organization. Second, leadership should develop a support base for decisions made in the context of projects and programs. In other words, leadership is a very functional concept according to HybridP3M, in which political dimensions such as self-interest are disregarded (for the sake of rationality). Only survival of the organization in a very competitive world counts, and therefore business success and growth are the main priority. In this chapter, the concept of organizational success is dissected (according to HybridP3M's interpretation), two main leadership styles are introduced (Burns 1978), and the notion of decision-making capability is introduced. Superior decision making equates making the right decisions. But in the context of groups, there is also an element of accountability for decision making, which needs to be taken into account. A successful organization consists of eight components which will be elaborated in the following subsections. The corresponding activities occur in no particular order. According to HybridP3M, leadership processes (not to be confused with formal leadership corresponding to management roles) are not necessarily restricted to key authorities. It follows from leadership theory that there is complex relationship between the leader and the follower. In this light, leadership processes transcend traditional lines of authority. Accordingly, leadership is not only a matter of power but also character, an opportunity for team dynamics in complex situations, and thus agile behavior.

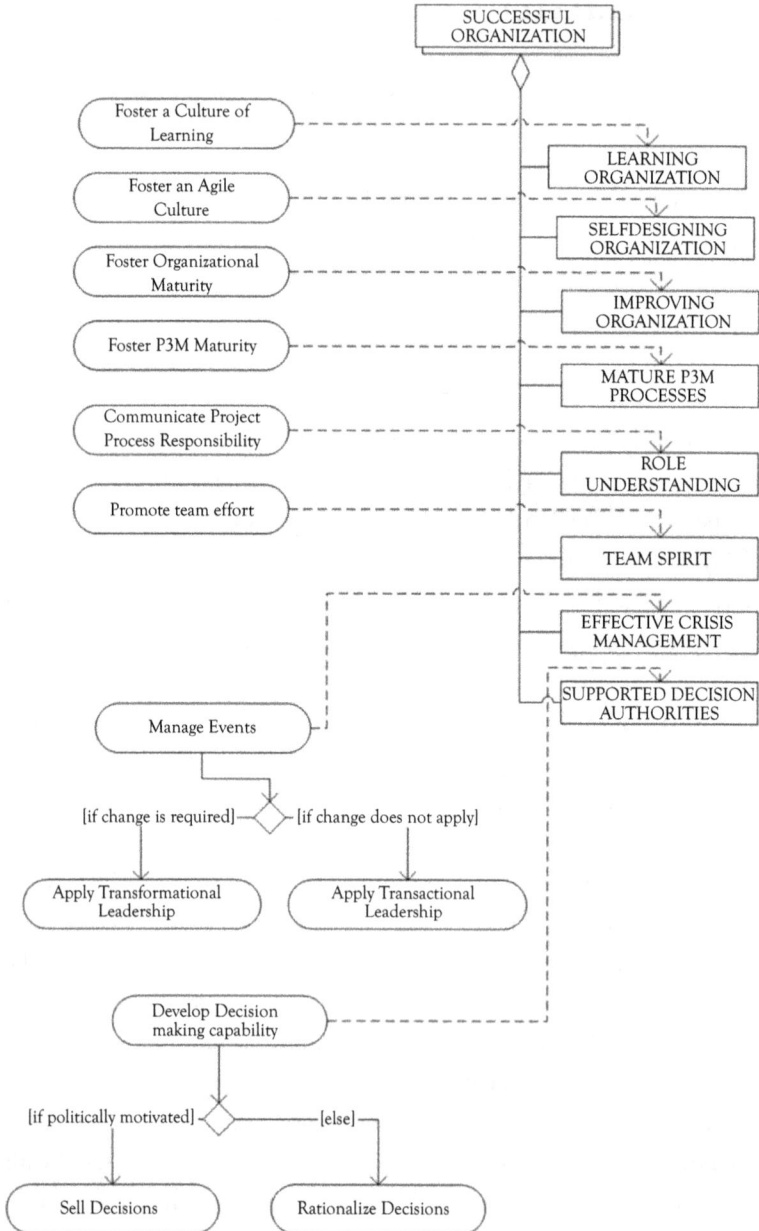

Figure 13.1 Leading the project or program PDD

Fostering a Culture of Learning

Fostering a culture of learning is essential in the context of developing a learning organization. One practical approach to this leadership process is to stimulate knowledge management, as learning is partially a function of knowledge integration and other knowledge processes. A second important aspect is to increase learning capability. In this light promotion of evaluation activity is key. Learning often takes place in the context of success and failure. It follows that failure and mistakes must be tolerated to some extent. From a long-term perspective, advocated here, blame should be restricted to situations in which mistakes are repeated but could have been prevented thanks to existing lessons learned or cases (describing similar situations), or sharing of tacit knowledge. Also, learning from success should not be taken for granted. In organizations, there are often barriers to learning, at various levels, across dimensions. Leadership implies making these barriers visible and overcoming them. In most cases, this involves cultural change, which is never easy to accomplish.

Fostering an Agile Culture

An agile culture is characterized by a widespread agile mindset, underlying particular behaviors. While the delivery model of any project or program is either predictive or Agile, depending on the type of project and industry, an agile mindset is beneficial either way, HybridP3M assumes. Agile project management, whether realistic and/or sound or not, is simply the new ideal. Projects and programs increasingly demand responsiveness to change, an agile feature. The latter is due to the dynamic character of projects and programs, which is commonly accepted. Arguably, projects and programs are becoming less and less predictive, irrespective of incremental and iterative delivery. Hence, the need for change management is universal. In order to foster an agile culture, leadership should concentrate on formal change management procedure and promote agile values, such as flexibility, customer satisfaction, customer intimacy, acceleration, and dynamic capability at any level. Undoubtedly, an agile culture contributes to a "self-designing organization" (Weick and Westley 1996), an effective organizational approach dealing with uncertainty.

Fostering Organizational Maturity

The activity to foster organizational maturity is a leadership process that is driven by capability maturity management. Gaining higher maturity levels is a key value in this context. In the ideal situation, the main goal, processes are optimized. In order to realize optimization of processes, however, it is essential to develop maturity across organizational dimensions (recall MAIDEO's five enterprise dimensions of an organization). Adopting a methodology like HybridP3M has implications not only for organization and process, but also for strategy and policy, monitoring and control, IT, and people and culture. Each of these areas should be developed and this requires leadership. That said, as project team members have limited corporate authority the main area in the context of projects and programs is arguably people and culture. By assuming leadership roles active members can stimulate each other with respect to personal growth, learning (including gaining knowledge and problem solving), and skills development. As a result, the outcome is an improving organization, essential in becoming a market leader.

Fostering P3M Maturity

By applying a P3M methodology like HybridP3M consistently across projects, project management team members lay the foundation for high P3M maturity levels. Application of HybridP3M's processes combined with understanding of process interfaces and interdependencies (in a P3M landscape), supported by never-ending accumulation of knowledge and experience, creates a path for optimization and sets the conditions for more success and less failure. Leadership should stress the importance of project assurance so that HybridP3M is indeed consistently applied. Second, leadership should facilitate understanding of P3M interfaces as an enterprise architecture view emerges among key staff. Third and finally, related to learning, P3M maturity depends on knowledge development and subsequent knowledge processes. So leadership should foster learning in every aspect of P3M.

Communicating Project Process Responsibility

Leadership also involves communicating project process responsibility in order to develop better role understanding across the team. Project process responsibility implies HybridP3M process understanding in a situated, practical setting. While HybridP3M provides a lot of guidance, using both explicit and implicit assumptions, it is the combination of matrices 1 to 3 that establishes roles and responsibilities and provides the basis for social contracts. It is unrealistic to assume that the ambiguous and complex nature of project processes will never result in organizational issues such as role disarray and general confusion. Therefore, leadership should resort to simple communication in order to prevent such issues. As HybridP3M believes in social contracts sustained by the right type of leadership and team dynamics, resorting to formal job descriptions, a PRINCE2 concept, should be exceptional (as a last resort rooted in follow-on actions).

Promoting Team Effort

The leadership process of promoting team effort is self-evident. Team spirit is an important foundation for achieving better results and efficient working. Project performance simply depends on team spirit. This is a matter of project establishment, getting the right group of people together, as well as team building. It is generally accepted that team building requires coaching. So leadership processes promoting team effort imply coaching ability, a skill that needs to be acknowledged, promoted, and trained. Team effort applies to the project management team, supervised by a project board and influenced by corporate/portfolio management, but also subteams of specialists headed by team managers.

Managing Events

Events relate to *new* situations that require human attention and which are not part of daily routine, such as work triggers or anticipated process transitions. There are two kinds of events: expected and unexpected. The main implication here is the level of possible preparation for events occurring. Note that preparation requires leadership skills. In the context of leadership, events may trigger conscious changes, set by the leadership. HybridP3M assumes that if change is required this calls for "transformational leadership," and if change does not apply "transactional leadership" should be used, two well-established leadership styles. In case of crisis, the ability to manage events may contribute to effective crisis management, another element of a successful organization.

Applying Transformational Leadership

Transformational leadership (Burns 1978) is based on a dynamic relationship between leader and follower in which both roles stimulate each other based on higher needs, such as morality, and assumes that values and assumptions are not fixed but can be influenced. Hence, this leadership style is in theory the right one for cultural change. Note that according to Schein (1985) values and assumptions lay at the heart of culture. Most cultural changes fail because leaders try to change artifacts and symbols, or patterns of behavior, without the means (or ideas) to foster change at a deeper level. That is to say, changing assumptions and values is fundamental to cultural change. Transformational leadership claims that if carried out effectively there is also less resistance to change. According to Bass (1995), transformational leadership has four dimensions:

1. *Idealized influence.* Effective transformational leaders have charisma. They are role models that followers want to identify with.
2. *Inspiration motivation.* An effective transformational leader inspires and motivates others. He or she is well capable of communicating his or her vision and followers do identify with this vision.
3. *Intellectual stimulation.* An effective transformational leader challenges followers intellectually and stimulates creativity, sometimes essential in problem solving.
4. *Individualized consideration.* An effective transformational leader understands the power of a collective, but at the same time has attention for the needs of individuals. He or she supervises, coaches, provides feedback, and acknowledges the needs of followers.

Applying Transactional Leadership

Transactional leadership is the type of leadership that is based on win–win situations and is effective when assumptions and values are fixed. An effective transactional leader gets things done in exchange for something. In other words, it is the type of leadership defined by incentives. Bass argues that the best leaders can switch between transformational and transactional leadership. As stated earlier, transactional leadership is most effective when change does not apply. It is the preferred leadership style while maintaining a status quo. Transactional leadership has two dimensions:

1. Contingent reward. An effective transactional leader sets targets, establishes expectations, and determines relevant reward for followers.
2. Management-by-exception. An effective transactional leader does not intervene as long as old methods are functional and followers keep realizing set targets in alignment with the established norms.

Developing Decision-Making Capability

The final element of a successful organization is supported decision authorities. When decision authorities are supported, decisions taken are respected and executed accordingly. This leads to stability and order, that is to say, a more effective management environment. In order to achieve this level of support, decision makers must build a reputation of sound leadership and accurate management. Ultimately, managers or leaders are judged by their decisions and their outcomes. Therefore, it is essential as a decision authority to develop "decision-making capability." Decision-making capability in its most effective form is interpreted as the ability to make the right decisions in the right setting following a decision-making process that can be justified in hindsight. As problems and issues tend to repeat across similar projects this calls for case-based reasoning (CBR), an analytical and rational form of decision making. The limitation of CBR is that it only applies to problem solving, not the whole spectrum of decision making. The whole spectrum of decision making covers also political decision making, which is inevitable. In case decisions are politically motivated, it is important to sell them (for buy-in). In case they are not driven by political motives it is key to rationalize them (also for greater commitment). The greater the understanding of sometimes controversial decisions the greater the tolerance, the stronger the reputation and so on.

Selling Decisions

Selling decisions is a typical political activity. It is mainly the domain of the bigger project/program sponsors and is driven by larger interests. Make-or-buy decisions like selecting a particular supplier, when objective procurement criteria do not apply, is a typical example. Promoting a project methodology to a third party (for integration purposes) is another example. By selling decisions, key decision makers show that they remain sensitive to reception, bearing in mind stakeholders' needs. By selling decisions, key decision makers can gain political power.

Rationalizing Decisions

Decision making should be as rational as possible. Rational decision making enables critique based on analytical grounds. This is important because decision makers are responsible and sometimes accountable for outcomes. Both success and failure need to be traced back to the original decision and/or taken actions. Only a rational approach contributes to the development of decision-making capability and long-term organizational learning, including learning from mistakes. Rationalization on hindsight of political decisions is not advocated and rather perverse as the related decision-making process was never analytical other than serving particular interests.

Process Aspects

Figure 13.2 captures the knowledge nature of leading the project or program.

$$\circledcirc -2 \quad \bigcirc -1 \quad \bigcirc 0 \quad \bigcirc 1 \quad \bigcirc 2$$

Figure 13.2 Tacit–explicit continuum of leading the project or program

Leadership depends on tacit knowledge. Explicit information only plays a support role, mainly for communication ends.

Figure 13.3 captures the manageability of leading the project or program.

$$\bigcirc \text{-2} \quad \bigcirc \text{-1} \quad \bigcirc \text{0} \quad \odot \text{1} \quad \bigcirc \text{2}$$

Figure 13.3 Step-by-step process versus skilled activity continuum of leading the project or program

While leadership is definitely not a step-by-step process that can be repeated, it is sensitive to corporate strategy and policy. Hence, it can be influenced and directed.

Figure 13.4 captures the specialization level of leading the project or program.

$$\odot \text{0} \quad \bigcirc \text{1} \quad \bigcirc \text{2} \quad \bigcirc \text{3} \quad \bigcirc \text{4}$$

Figure 13.4 Management–specialist continuum of leading the project or program

Leadership is a management skill; it is not a specialization confined to a particular role.

Figure 13.5 captures IT support in relation to integrating leading the project or program.

$$\odot \text{0} \quad \bigcirc \text{1} \quad \bigcirc \text{2} \quad \bigcirc \text{3} \quad \bigcirc \text{4}$$

Figure 13.5 Available IT support for leading the project or program

Leadership is a human quality; it does not rely on IT.

Figure 13.6 captures the complexity of integrating knowledge management.

$$\bigcirc \text{0} \quad \bigcirc \text{1} \quad \bigcirc \text{2} \quad \bigcirc \text{3} \quad \odot \text{4}$$

Figure 13.6 Task complexity scale of leading the project or program

Leadership is a very complex process simply based on the complex relationship between leader and followers.

MAIDEO Requirements

Table 13.1 presents MAIDEO requirements related to "leading the project/program."

*Table 13.1 MAIDEO requirements related to leading the project/
program*

Requirement	Level	Dimension
Leadership takes into account crisis management.	1	People and culture
Depending on the political nature, decisions are sold to those affected.	1	People and culture
Team effort is promoted.	2	People and culture
Transactional leadership is applied when status quo does not need to be challenged.	2	People and culture
Project process responsibility is communicated continuously.	3	People and culture
Status quo is challenged based on transformational leadership.	3	People and culture
To become a learning organization is part of the corporate mission, vision, and strategy.	4	Strategy and policy
Leaders foster an agile culture.	4	People and culture
Depending on the political nature, decisions are rationalized.	4	People and culture
Leaders foster a culture of learning.	5	People and culture
Leaders are driven to improve organizational maturity.	5	People and culture
Senior management is driven to improve decision-making capability across projects and programs.	5	Strategy and policy

CHAPTER 14

Project/Program Establishment

Project/program establishment is an organizational theme (see Figure 14.1). It is the least complex HybridP3M process, yet has a profound impact on projects and programs. Establishment is concerned with management positions as well as selecting the right staff consisting of various specialists. Establishment highly depends on the matrix approach of HybridP3M, elaborated in Chapter 2. This matrix approach identifies the organizational structure of the management team, divides roles, and suggests process responsibility tied to roles. Building on the adopted matrices, establishment deals with selecting the right people for the right job. HybridP3M's project/program establishment process is characterized by the active role of process champions, who may be external people, and the acknowledgment of the importance of team building. Essentially, establishment is a corporate solution based on corporate management and corporate policies. But developing successful teams takes experience and depends on a larger pool of available resources. On Jobboard4Projects, a solution is explored that is characterized by global resource management, utilizing external talents to join new projects and programs, according to resourcing needs. This solution is called the "project formation tool" or "team formation" and also supports the business logic as implied by the matrix approach, characteristic for HybridP3M.

Identifying Project Board Members

The project board is by definition a layer above the project management team. To avoid confusion, in HybridP3M this excludes the project manager. This management layer is responsible for project direction. Project board membership should reflect various project or program interest groups. In general, the project board consists of sponsors and senior stakeholders.

Figure 14.1 Project/program establishment PDD

With regard to the specific roles, the actual composition, it depends on the situation. The PRINCE2 distinction between executive, senior supplier, and senior user is considered not generic enough. Depending on the customer–supplier environment, there is, however, only one project board at the project level, responsible for the entire project. In this context, there is a customer who holds the main business case. This customer is represented by an executive or similar role. The executive acts on behalf of the senior responsible owner of the enterprise—not necessarily a single corporation—behind the project or program. On the other hand, there could be multiple suppliers, responsible for only a specific segment of the total life cycle—being less significant. This means that a senior supplier role cannot be taken for granted. The senior user role, in turn, depends on the type of project and industry. In case of software development, including Agile delivery, the user plays a central role. It should be stressed that not every project board member has the same decision authority in terms of power. For example, some stakeholders (with a smaller stake or share), invited to join the board, could have a more advisory or support function.

Appointing Project Management Team

The appointment of the project management team follows Matrix 1 in which HybridP3M roles are mapped with processes. This mapping contains important information on process responsibility and thereby provides an understanding of role requirements. In the ideal situation, every distinguished role is taken by a different individual, specialized in a particular role. In practice, available resources may not allow that. In those cases, it is inevitable that HybridP3M roles are combined. This is a form of scaling the methodology. On the project management team, the project manager could be considered the generalist, whereas all the other roles are specializations. HybridP3M highly recommends not to combine the role of project knowledge manager, which is key in knowledge-intensive projects. This role requires unique skills and a thorough understanding of knowledge management, a unique field of study and interest, and a management discipline on its own. In a corporate portfolio, appointment of management roles also depends on Matrix 2, which has implications for resource availability. The various HybridP3M management roles call for new specialization.

Connecting with Organizational Process Champions

Every project management role should have contact with more experienced members in an organization for learning and growth. Many, if not most, companies have addressed this aspect of socialization, at some point in their history, using various organizational interventions with or without the support of ICT. In addition to corporate solutions, HybridP3M stresses the importance of process champions as key contacts. Every HybridP3M process corresponds to a subfunction, which is also a knowledge domain. Every single HybridP3M knowledge domain should develop process champions over time, based on personal ambition and organizational direction. And it is in the interest of the organization that these champions share their knowledge and experience with less experienced staff. Knowledge brokering, a ProwLO concept, is a mechanism, an intentional procedure, to connect project members with process champions in the context of solving knowledge/experience gaps. But connecting with organizational process champions should also be a natural process, part of the organizational culture.

Appointing Specialists

Appointing specialists is part of resource management as generally practiced by organizations. Companies have developed their own methods and approaches for selecting the right team members. However, they rely on a limited pool of available people. Ideally, the right talents are selected disregarding organizational background, from a larger pool of resources. External specialists should play a greater role in team formation based on temporary or freelance contracts. This requires a new approach for recruitment, namely a global recruitment process based on dynamic opportunity as envisioned by Jobboard4Projects, relying on a highly skilled, flexible workforce of knowledge workers, called Knowmads (Moravec 2013).

Investing in Team Building

The final activity of project/program establishment is to invest in team building. It is beyond the scope of HybridP3M to go into detail here. Other work should complement HybridP3M with regard to team building. The key is that organizations should invest in this process depending on their own unique vision, addressing multiple aspects such as remote working, conflict resolution, productivity, team learning, and team spirit. For example, Peter Senge has stated a few interesting things regarding team learning. According to Senge, a great team is characterized by the following:

- To function and perform in an extraordinary manner
- To trust each other and complement one another
- To have common goals that are more important than individual goals

Process Aspects

Figure 14.2 captures the knowledge nature of project/program establishment

$\bigcirc$ -2 $\bigcirc$ -1 $\circledcirc$ 0 $\bigcirc$ 1 $\bigcirc$ 2

Figure 14.2 Tacit–explicit continuum of project/program establishment

Establishment has both significant tacit and explicit dimensions. Tacit knowledge is dominant in the associated people management theme, whereas explicit knowledge is key in understanding profiles of people for effective resource management.

Figure 14.3 captures the manageability of project/program establishment.

$$\odot\text{-2} \quad \bigcirc\text{-1} \quad \bigcirc\text{0} \quad \bigcirc\text{1} \quad \bigcirc\text{2}$$

Figure 14.3 Step-by-step process versus skilled activity continuum of project/program establishment

Establishment is highly manageable. Corporate standards combined with corporate strategy and policy are dominant here.

Figure 14.4 captures the specialization level of project/program establishment.

$$\odot\text{0} \quad \bigcirc\text{1} \quad \bigcirc\text{2} \quad \bigcirc\text{3} \quad \bigcirc\text{4}$$

Figure 14.4 Management–specialist continuum of project/program establishment

Establishment is typical, generic management work. It is not performed by specialists.

Figure 14.5 captures IT support in relation to project/program establishment.

$$\bigcirc\text{0} \quad \bigcirc\text{1} \quad \bigcirc\text{2} \quad \odot\text{3} \quad \bigcirc\text{4}$$

Figure 14.5 Available IT support for project/program establishment

Establishment is supported by existing tools in the sense that they administer team membership. But this is a limited area of the whole concept. Resource management can rely on clever use of spreadsheets. The selection of the right people to join a project may depend on innovative resourcing. For example, Jobboard4Projects has introduced global resource management based on dynamic opportunity, using extensive profile information such as Candidate Pages.

Figure 14.6 captures the complexity of project/program establishment.

$$\bigcirc\text{0} \quad \bigcirc\text{1} \quad \odot\text{2} \quad \bigcirc\text{3} \quad \bigcirc\text{4}$$

Figure 14.6 Task complexity scale of project/program establishment

Establishment is not really a complex process but requires occasional expert judgment and gut feeling.

MAIDEO Requirements

Table 14.1 presents MAIDEO requirements related to "project/program establishment."

Table 14.1 *MAIDEO requirements related to project/program establishment*

Requirement	Level	Dimension
Team building is acknowledged as a key success factor.	1	People and culture
Specialists are appointed based on their skills and other profile requirements.	1	People and culture
The project management team is based on HybridP3M's matrices 1 and 2.	2	Organization and process
Role responsibilities are based on all three of HybridP3M's matrices.	2	Organization and process
Organizational champions play a significant role in project processes.	3	People and culture
The composition of project board membership is flexible according to project or program needs.	3	Organization and process
The senior responsible owner is officially represented by the executive on the project board.	4	Organization and process
The project knowledge manager role is not combined with other management roles.	4	People and culture
Resource management uses global resource management solutions based on dynamic opportunity.	5	IT
"The establishment aspect" of project organization is considered when forming new teams, including subaspects such as PR, representing interests, use of social media.	5	People and culture

CHAPTER 15

Providing Assurance

Project/program assurance is based on the need to provide confidence in the face of uncertainty (see Figure 15.1). In the context of projects, it has been made more popular by, for example, PRINCE2. In PRINCE2, project assurance is a subfunction of project direction, a project board responsibility sometimes delegated as a distinct role. In reality, project/ program assurance is a very broad concept, as noted by Onna and Koning (2004). According to these authors, assurance covers most if not all stakeholders' needs, a rather vague assumption. The specific examples they provide, following the PRINCE2 standard, include monitoring the business case, correct use of standards, customer satisfaction, correct use of resources, and noticing scope creep. Based on the meaning of assurance and such examples one can imagine the importance of an assurance process, but it must be more specific. Assurance should also interfaces with change management, which enables improvements according to a long-term enterprise perspective. HybridP3M's approach is partly based on the unpublished work of Jim Livesey, a consultant who once posted key reasons for using independent assurance. Three of these reasons are adopted or adapted as part of the HybridP3M assurance process. Providing assurance is closely related to project evaluation, but it has clearly different process goals and a different activity flow, as depicted in Figure 14.1. As a process, providing assurance is quite straightforward, and thus the explanation of individual activities in this context is rather short.

Assessing Process Consistency Against Corporate Standards

The first activity of providing assurance introduced here is to assess process consistency against corporate standards. It is a continuous activity, in principle not bound by life cycle dynamics. But like any other form of evaluation, it requires time to run and, hence, most likely occurs at the end

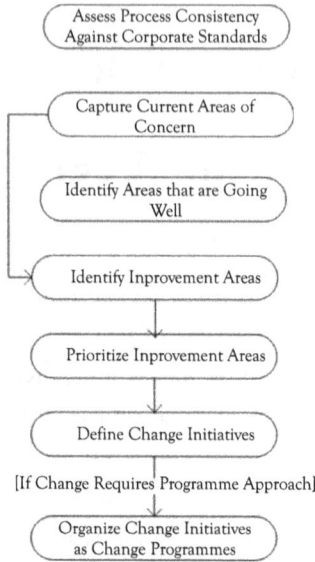

Figure 15.1 Providing assurance PDD

of stages, other decision moments, or handover of key deliverables, which according to Livesey correspond to key times to run independent assurance. It should be noted that this activity is inspired by PRINCE2 guidance. One practical approach is to focus on missing activity, as prescribed according to the process model, with or without lifecycle management extension (i.e., mapping with PRINCE2). A noteworthy best practice in the interest of project assurance is to motivate project management team members to define process goals when adopting the HybridP3M process model.

Capturing Current Areas of Concern

Capturing current areas of concern is adapted from Livesey who used the word validated in this context. The issue with validating is that project assurance may be the first function to discover an area of concern. Areas of concern are instrumental in ad hoc guidance, a key project board responsibility.

Identifying Areas That Are Going Well

Identifying areas that are going well is typical for holistic evaluation, looking at the negative as well as positive things. The insights and lessons learned in this context provide useful input for project evaluation. This activity is adopted from the work by Livesey.

Identifying Improvement Areas

Identifying improvement areas follows the activity to capture current areas of concern and is adopted from the work by Livesey as well. The former activity involves a systematic analysis of issues that tend to repeat. Issues that are systematic should be on a priority list for necessary changes. The development of such a list is the next, follow-up activity.

Prioritizing Improvement Areas

Based on systematic issues, a priority list for necessary changes is developed. As part of this process, improvement areas are prioritized.

Defining Change Initiatives

Based on the analysis of improvement areas, project assurance next defines change initiatives at the corporate level. The definition of such change activity is then passed on to the corporate change management function for feedback and transfer of ownership (of the change issue).

Organizing Change Initiatives as Change Programs

Organizing change initiatives as change programs follows the definition of change initiatives and only applies if the desired change needs to be organized as a change program. That is only the case when dealing with complex changes. This final activity of project assurance is performed by the change management function as the start of new change management initiatives. The change management function relies on the project assurance function for a program mandate, provided in the context of a project or program.

Process Aspects

Figure 15.2 captures the knowledge nature of providing assurance.

○ -2 ○ -1 ○ 0 ◉ 1 ○ 2

Figure 15.2 Tacit–explicit continuum of providing assurance

Assurance tends to focus on explicit knowledge, but the tacit dimension cannot be ignored totally. Externalization, however, is a dominant theme.

Figure 15.3 captures the manageability of providing assurance.

◉ -2 ○ -1 ○ 0 ○ 1 ○ 2

Figure 15.3 Step-by-step process versus skilled activity continuum of providing assurance

Assurance advocates process consistency. Hence, assurance should be incorporated into corporate standards.

Figure 15.4 captures the specialization level of providing assurance.

○ -2 ◉ -1 ○ 0 ○ 1 ○ 2

Figure 15.4 Management–specialist continuum of providing assurance

Assurance is rather a generic management skill, not so much a specialization.

Figure 15.5 captures IT support in relation to providing assurance.

○ 0 ◉ 1 ○ 2 ○ 3 ○ 4

Figure 15.5 Available IT support for providing assurance

IT support mainly plays a role in ensuring process consistency. This is achieved thanks to the promotion of corporate standards and knowledge integration of process knowledge.

Figure 15.6 captures the complexity of providing assurance.

○ 0 ◉ 1 ○ 2 ○ 3 ○ 4

Figure 15.6 Task complexity scale of providing assurance

Once internalized, assurance is not a complex process.

MAIDEO Requirements

Table 15.1 presents MAIDEO requirements related to "providing assurance."

Table 15.1 MAIDEO requirements related to providing assurance

Requirement	Level	Dimension
Assurance takes into account process consistency based on corporate standards.	1	Organization and process
Current areas of concern are captured by assurance.	1	Organization and process
Improvement areas are identified.	2	Organization and process
Areas that are going well are identified.	2	Organization and process
Improvement areas are prioritized.	3	Organization and process
Changed initiatives are defined based on prioritized improvement areas.	3	Organization and process
Change initiatives are organized together with the corporate change management function.	4	Organization and process
Process consistency is enforced by assurance.	4	Monitoring and control
Improvement areas are taken seriously by corporate or portfolio management.	5	Strategy and policy
The assurance function takes care of a project or program mandate that triggers new change initiatives.	5	Organization and process

CHAPTER 16

Agile Product Delivery

Agile product delivery is the interplay between monitoring and control and at the project level, monitoring and control at the product delivery level, and system engineering (characterizing the specialist domain) (see Figure 16.1). Monitoring and control at the project level follows the stage-gate paradigm of HybridP3M and is a project management layer. Monitoring and control at the product delivery level deals with work packages and is a team management layer below the project management layer. These two processes are inspired by both PRINCE2 (i.e., controlling a stage and managing product delivery) and the Praxis framework (i.e., delivery process and development process), which have a similar approach to the management of work packages. Combined, the two monitoring and control processes capture a simple loop representing the flow of work packages. This loop can be repeated by new work triggers calling for additional work packages. System engineering includes specialist development work and other activities that contribute to the integrity of the end product. It is extreme, excluding any kind of unnecessary overhead, and inspired by Extreme Programming. So Agile product delivery is contextual and situated, not a superficial or simple Agile approach. The added value of monitoring and control at the project level is management control. The added value of monitoring and control at the product delivery level is controlled work execution. And the extreme approach to system engineering adds to agility. In this chapter, all three core process groups are elaborated without going into too much detail of every activity. The actual workflow can be derived from Figure 16.1.

Monitoring and Controland at the Project Level

Monitoring and control at the project level starts when the project manager authorizes a work package (triggering "authorize work" adopted from

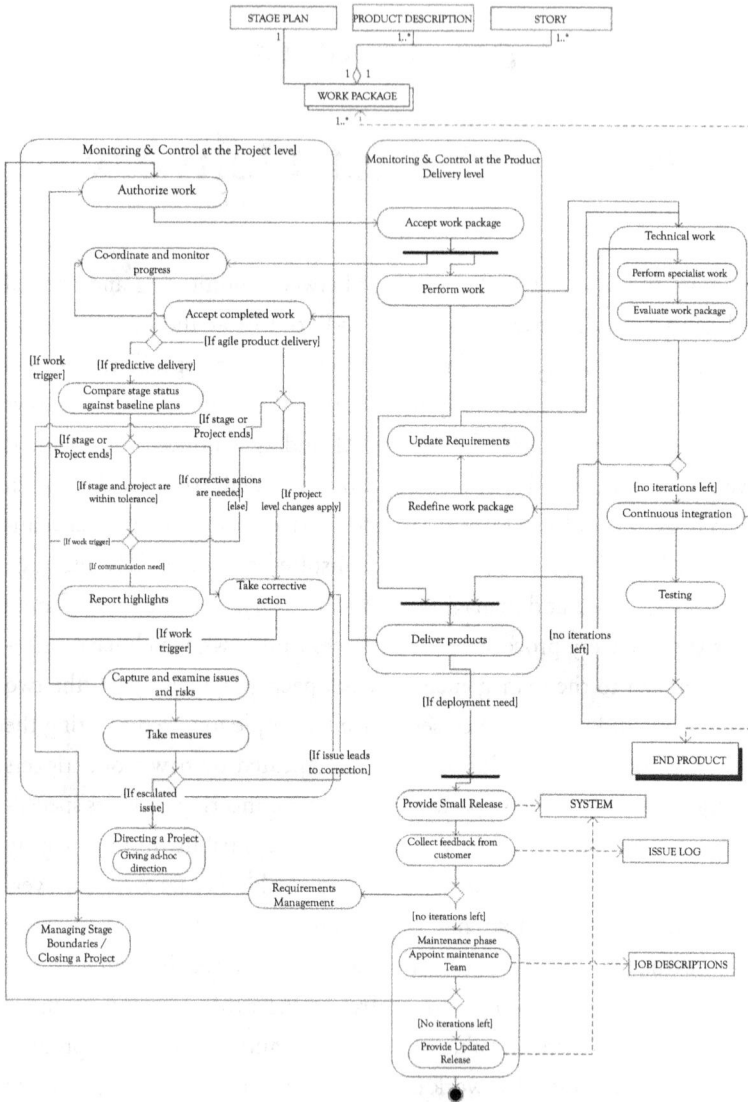

Figure 16.1 Agile product delivery PDD

Praxis framework). The follow-up activity is "coordinate and monitor progress," also adopted from Praxis, a more comprehensive counterpart of "review work package status" in PRINCE2. That is to say, "coordinate and monitor progress" follows work package execution or is triggered when completed work packages are received by the project manager. The next activity depends on the type of product delivery (delivery mode): predictive or Agile. This split is represented by a decision in the flow of activity as can be noted in Figure 16.1 (see the "decision diamond" that follows "co-ordinate and monitor progress"). In case of predictive delivery, the next activity is "compare stage status against baselines plans" (the PRINCE2 equivalent is "review the stage status"). Here the project manager (or controller) is dealing with management-by-exception. In case of Agile delivery, on the other hand, another decision follows. There are three decision outcomes here: (1) the stage or project ends (by whatever reason), (2) project-level changes apply, or (3) anything else. Note that "decision diamonds" not necessarily represent decision moments; more important are the unique conditions that lay out a path in terms of workflow. The first option leads to a boundaries process, for example, the PRINCE2 process of managing stage boundaries or, alternatively, closing a project. The second option plays an essential role in Agile project management as the project management team needs to anticipate change (a case for Agile project management). If project-level changes apply, the next activity is to take corrective action. Following corrective action, a work trigger may follow reinitiating the authorization of work, the beginning of a new loop. The third option, anything else, merges with another distinct decision diamond (see Figure 16.1). Back to predictive delivery, what follows "compare stage status against baseline plans" is a similar decision diamond with three options: (1) the stage or project ends, (2) stage or project is within tolerance, or (3) corrective actions are needed. The first option, just like in Agile delivery, leads to a boundaries process. The second option leads to a new decision diamond, either a new work trigger or the activity of "report highlights" based on communication needs. And the third option leads to "take corrective action," relevant in both scenarios (predictive and Agile) but based on different needs (predictive capability versus agility). Finally, there are two more independent activities in monitoring and control at the project level, namely "capture and examine issues and risks," adopted from PRINCE2, and "take measures," triggered by the former. These two activities are more continuous in nature. Note that "capture and examine issues and risks" may result in a work trigger. Taking measures may imply taking corrective action or result in escalation. In case of escalation, there is an interface with directing a project, calling for "give ad-hoc direction" (by the project board), a PRINCE2 activity. In conclusion, monitoring and control at the project level is partly a flexible process that can be adjusted according to a predictive or Agile delivery mode.

Monitoring and Control at the Product Delivery Level

The process of monitoring and control at the product delivery level starts with accepting a work package, which is triggered by the project manager who authorizes new work packages to the team manager. Following this, the work package is executed. After completion, the work package is delivered to the project manager, who is the receiver of the completed work package. Compared to PRINCE2 and Praxis framework equivalent, HybridP3M's monitoring and control process includes two additional activities. The first one is to redefine a work package. This activity interfaces with system engineering. When technical specialists perform specialist work, they end up with evaluating the assigned work package. Based on actual development work, as work execution unfolds, they may conclude that the currently defined work package does not correspond well to actual delivery. For example, implemented features and lower-level requirements may differ from planned features or requirements. In that case they provide feedback to the team manager, who may redefine the work package based on this new input. The second activity that follows is to update the requirements based on changes. These two new activities make work packages, and thus the management of product delivery, more agile. Monitoring and control at the product delivery level, combined with extreme system engineering discussed next, is both incremental and iterative, another Agile characteristic.

System Engineering

In today's business, system engineering is one of the most common project and program types. Therefore, this domain is used as the starting point for Agile product delivery. For other types of projects and programs, more focused on intangible project outcomes like change or capability development, this system engineering approach has limited use, but nonetheless may provide inspiration. Also civil engineering projects may greatly benefit from a system engineering approach, having similar technical phases (like gathering of requirements, design, construction, etc.). Technical work is triggered by the activity of performing work (adopted from Praxis framework), controlled by the team manager. Technical work consists mainly of domain-specific specialist work (like designing, programming, etc.). In addition, technical work implies evaluation of the work package issued by the team manager. The latter activity provides an interface to monitoring and control at the product delivery level, namely redefining a work package. This interface supports multiple (agile) iterations in the context of one work package, with redefinitions. If there are no more iterations, what follows is continuous integration. Continuous integration ensures that the technical work related to the current work package is integrated with the rest of the system, possibly the end product. This may require some form of configuration management like version control, as popularized by PRINCE2. After continuous integration follows testing. In an Agile setting, testing is a rather continuous process, not a separate technical phase later in the development cycle. Testing may trigger another iteration to perform specialist work again. This could be caused by the need to make improvements or rework. If testing does not trigger new iterations, especially when the new functionality has gained user acceptance (in a demo environment), it is safe to trigger the delivery of the work package, ending the cycle. User involvement is not always the case, however, at this stage as testing is usually performed by specialists. After the delivery of products, there might be a need for deployment. If that is the case, the next activity is to provide a small release (of the system or component). Following this, the customer is expected to provide feedback, which is collected in an issue log. Based on this information, requirements management is triggered based on new customer wishes. Requirements management, in turn, may trigger the definition of new work packages or modification of existing ones. Hence, another iteration may follow beginning with the activity to authorize a new work package by the project manager. Finally, when there are no more iterations left in the context of stages and the project as a whole, the project life cycle ends and marks the transition to the maintenance phase as part of a product life cycle. Note that with the advent of DevOps, the ending of the project life cycle might be blurred. The first activity in the context of the maintenance phase is to appoint a maintenance team to continue work on the product and its features. Following it are new iterations, again starting with the activity to authorize work packages, repeating the management and development cycle. So even after project completion, the principle of management by stages holds. If there are no more iterations left over a certain time span, the final activity is to provide an updated release. Based on this description and as you can read from the diagram, Agile product delivery is highly iterative and thus agile, yet a controlled process.

Process Aspects

Figure 16.2 captures the knowledge nature of Agile product delivery.

$$\bigcirc \text{-2} \quad \bigcirc \text{-1} \quad \bigcirc \text{0} \quad \circledcirc \text{1} \quad \bigcirc \text{2}$$

Figure 16.2 Tacit–explicit continuum of Agile product delivery

From a process perspective, delivery depends on explicit process knowledge. The specialist activities as part of delivery also involve a great deal of tacit knowledge.

Figure 16.3 captures the manageability of Agile product delivery.

$$\circledcirc \text{-2} \quad \bigcirc \text{-1} \quad \bigcirc \text{0} \quad \bigcirc \text{1} \quad \bigcirc \text{2}$$

Figure 16.3 Step-by-step process versus skilled activity continuum of Agile product delivery

Although HybridP3M's delivery process is complex, the related work-flow can be managed and standardized.

Figure 16.4 captures the specialization level of Agile product delivery.

$$\bigcirc \text{-2} \quad \bigcirc \text{-1} \quad \bigcirc \text{0} \quad \circledcirc \text{1} \quad \bigcirc \text{2}$$

Figure 16.4 Management–specialist continuum of Agile product delivery

Delivery management, disregarding specialist work, is rather a team effort performed by the project manager and team manager(s). The team management aspect of delivery is arguably a specialization. In practice, how-ever, the team manager role can be combined with the project manager role.

Figure 16.5 captures IT support in relation to Agile product delivery.

$$\bigcirc \text{0} \quad \bigcirc \text{1} \quad \bigcirc \text{2} \quad \circledcirc \text{3} \quad \bigcirc \text{4}$$

Figure 16.5 Available IT support for Agile product delivery

Delivery can be supported by task management software or workflow management solutions. While beneficial in some cases, software is not essential.

Figure 16.6 captures the complexity of Agile product delivery.

$$\bigcirc 0 \quad \bigcirc 1 \quad \bigcirc 2 \quad \bigcirc 3 \quad \circledcirc 4$$

Figure 16.6 Task complexity scale of Agile product delivery

Given the combination of monitoring and control at the project and delivery levels, and all specialist activities, delivery is a very complex process. It is even more complex given the incremental and iterative nature of system development.

MAIDEO Requirements

Table 16.1 presents MAIDEO requirements related to "Agile product delivery."

Table 16.1 MAIDEO requirements related to Agile product delivery

Requirement	Level	Dimension
Agile delivery is the interplay between monitoring and control at project level, monitoring and control at the delivery level, and specialist work.	1	Organization and process
The project manager is involved with delivery based on the PRINCE2 controlling a stage process.	1	Organization and process
Monitoring and Control at the delivery level is based on the corresponding PRINCE2 process, dealing with work packages.	2	Organization and process
Agile delivery is based on the system engineering paradigm based on the type of project or program.	2	Organization and process
Work packages are redefined based on feedback from specialists.	3	Organization and process
Delivery is both incremental and iterative, even in more predictive environments.	3	Organization and process
The maintenance phase follows seamlessly project or program end.	4	Organization and process
The customer plays a key role in Agile delivery.	4	People and culture
Specialists critically evaluate work packages.	5	People and culture
Delivery is characterized by testing and continuous integration with the right people for testing (specialist testers).	5	Organization and process

Conclusion

The goal of this book is to introduce and describe a new methodology for hybrid project and program management. Projects and programs are treated similarly based on the assumption that their distinction is artificial in the first place. What constitutes a project or program is defined by work and how it is organized. The functional processes (following HybridP3M) and life cycle phases (adopted from, e.g., PRINCE2) that apply to this organization are identical for projects and programs. Only the work itself is defined differently, resulting in different project and program types. In the name of HybridP3M, there is also a reference to P3M, not to provide a solution for hybrid portfolio management but to stress the non-standalone character of projects. Projects are situated and subject to various external factors. A better understanding of the environment of projects is critical in order to predict success or failure.

One way to better understand the environment and external factors is by maturity assessment. In this book, a new maturity framework was introduced, namely "Maturity Alignment In Dimensions of Enterprise Origin," in short MAIDEO. Recall that MAIDEO consists of five aspects or organizational dimensions: (1) strategy and policy, (2) organization and process, (3) monitoring and control, (4) people and culture, and (5) IT. Scheper (2002) has found that better organizational performance depends on not only higher maturity levels but also alignment across the five dimensions, a unique insight from business and IT alignment literature. Together with the specific maturity requirements provided in each process chapter, this book provides guidance and helps to define a roadmap for improvement. Developing the organization toward higher maturity levels while seeking alignment is called capability maturity management, a cross-functional area targeting various organizational stakeholders, and unmistakably a P3M challenge.

Knowledge-based project management, advocated in this book, requires process support in the area of knowledge management. In HybridP3M, this support consists of a designated process called "integrating knowledge management" and a number of principles. Focusing on the role of specialist knowledge managers, integrating knowledge management is complex as it aligns with the ProwLO methodology, which is an advanced work in the field of project knowledge management. The profound Knowmadic steps technique for knowledge integration, part of it, is also challenging due to its complexity and abstract concepts. The associated learning curve depends on an effective use of KnowledgePlace, companion software. In the light of project excellence, it is advocated that knowledge management is part of the overall project management process. Like ProwLO itself, it involves many actors. However, the functional achievement of integrating knowledge management mainly depends on a proficient project knowledge manager and a knowledgeable project manager.

HybridP3M is a hybrid methodology for project and program management. What makes it hybrid is mainly the combination of Agile product delivery with more traditional processes, as reflected by implicit, traditional process goals (implicit because they depend on project definition, that is, actual implementation of the method in practice). Effectively the traditional processes form an overarching framework for Agile delivery (at lower level), just as happened with PRINCE2-Agile but with a different implementation. Hybrid project management is not a hybrid form of delivery mode, which remains a binary option: predictive or Agile. Delivery basically depends on the required solution, project characteristics, and the management environment in general. HybridP3M favors agile delivery for the sake of agile benefits and has organized Agile product delivery accordingly. HybridP3M's Agile product delivery is characterized by a work package process for greater management control (aligned with PRINCE2), focuses on system engineering, and is inspired by Extreme Programming. Furthermore, HybridP3M promotes a joint responsibility for project processes. This is arguably an Agile approach, lessening the management overhead for project managers. Finally, in terms of principles, HybridP3M promotes an agile mindset while complementing a culture of management control. Although it is difficult to categorize principles along the Agile–traditional dichotomy, the latter principle captures the very essence of hybrid.

Part of HybridP3M are three matrices. Matrices 1 and 3 are part of project definition (see Chapter 3). Matrix 1 consolidates project roles in relation to processes, based on a joint process responsibility. Matrix 3 is a project management exercise in which functional processes are mapped with life cycle processes. Basically, it is a mapping between HybridP3M and PRINCE2 or an alternative life cycle management approach. Creating Matrix 3 is an act of (personal) knowledge mastery. On Insight Intranet there is a section (HybridP3M Matrix 3) that enables users to relate process knowledge via the medium of transfers (max. 500 character posts, derived from the notion of "Knowledge Transfer") to "entries" in which functional processes come together with PRINCE2 life cycle processes (i.e., phases) in a two-dimensional grid. These entries are project-specific, that is, unique for actual projects in which the user is engaged in, and user-specific (private knowledge). It should be noted that the practical implementation of HybridP3M may differ per project (due to tailoring, scaling, or simply more focus in certain areas) and thus drives unique insights and other knowledge (one specific example is the combined process goals). Finally, Matrix 2 is a solution for corporate resource management taking into account a portfolio of projects and project roles, combined with the knowledge that roles can be combined by single actors, notwithstanding some exceptions.

In the Introduction, it was stated that agility is a variable, depending on management overhead and flexible delivery (or anticipated change in programs). This means it is a trade-off. Generally, it can be argued that traditional methods lack flexible delivery, while agile methods lack management overhead (and thus lack control). HybridP3M lies somewhere in the golden middle, depending on its practical implementation. The selected delivery mode, either predictive or agile, as part of the Project Approach, reinforces this trade-off. Accordingly, hybrid project management always seeks to find the right balance between control and flexibility given the presented situation, including unique project characteristics. Therefore, hybrid project management is above all a very pragmatic approach using the best of what already exists, blending traditional management with agile traditions, in an innovative way.

APPENDIX

Cases-Method

Figure A.1 represents the Cases-method as adopted from Rosinski (2019).

In this Appendix the essence of the Cases-method is captured. A step-by-step explanation and more background information can be found in Rosinski (2019). Essentially, managerial events are often repetitive cycles of decision–implementation–feedback–decision. New iterations may start when the initial problem has not been solved (or only partly) or when a new problem has arisen due to project behavior (Rosinski 2019, 85). A cross-reference to the Cases-method is important because the impact of decision making on project behavior should be analyzed. Decision rationale, actual outcomes, and derived lessons are relevant in the context of not only project knowledge management (for the capture of cases, a key knowledge type, and artefact) but also project management, in particular management intervention (with or without case-based reasoning support).

The method is unique for many reasons. It takes into account emergent and situational factors that explain the original problem. Emergent factors are unpredicted circumstances, often caused by various events. Situational factors can be predicted or identified upfront. In other words, the causes of the problem are made more distinct. Second, an effort is made to establish causality between taken decisions and/or actions and actual project behavior, explaining outcomes. Third, comments are captured on the decision-making process in order to indicate bounded rationality, lack of information, poor communication, political motives, etc. Fourth, a distinction is made between easy lessons learned and hard lessons learned, depending on complex causal relationships. Fifth and finally, the Cases-method captures metadata such as related knowledge domain and knowledge areas.

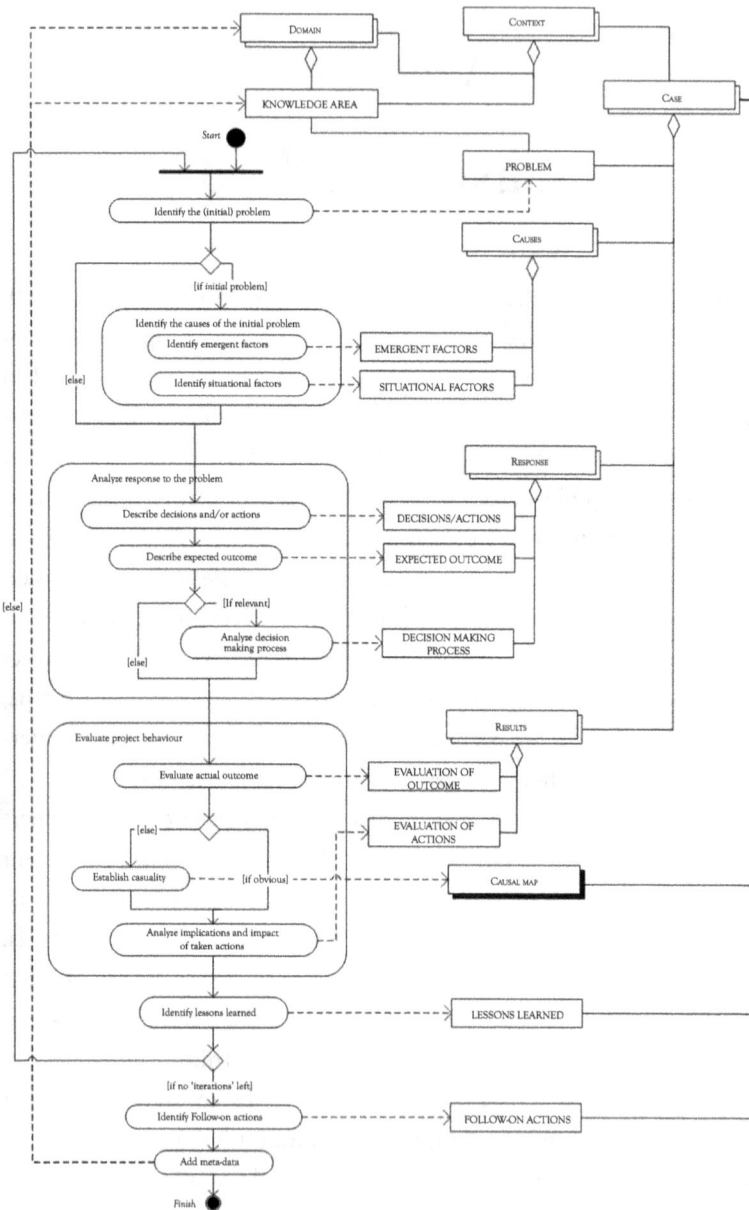

Figure A.1 Cases-method

Source: Adopted from Rosinski (2019), p. 82.

References

Archibald, R. 2004. "Project Management State of the Art 2004." http://maxwideman.com/guests/stateofart/organizations.htm (accessed December 12, 2007).

BA-Experts. 2016. "What Exactly Is Requirements Elicitation." https://youtube.com/watch?v=vSXn16qMEZo (accessed August 20, 2020).

Barnes, M. 2002. "A Long Term View of Project Management—Its Past and its Likely Future." www.pmforum.org/library/papers/2002/longtermpmbarnes.pdf (accessed June 25, 2007).

Bass, B.M. 1995. "Theory of Transformational Leadership Redux." *Leadership Quarterly* 6, pp. 463–478.

Brolsma, D., and M. Kouwenhoven. 2019. *MSP® Foundation Programme Management Courseware*. Amsterdam: Van Haren Publishing B.V.

Burns, J.M. 1978. *Leadership*. New York, NY: Harper & Row.

Chatterjee, A. 2020. *Insight by John Dewey*. LinkedIn Timeline.

Department of Finance. 2020. "Identifying and Structuring Programme and Project Benefits." https://finance-ni.gov.uk/articles/identifying-and-structuring-programme-and-project-benefits (accessed August 20, 2020).

Eden, C., T. Williams, F. Ackermann, and S. Howick. 2000. "The Role of Feedback Dynamics in Disruption and Delay on the Nature of Disruption and Delay (D&D) in Major Projects." *The Journal of the Operational Research Society* 51, no. 3, 291–300.

Franken, A. 2016. "Benefits Management: Who cares?" https://slideshare.net/assocpm/benefits-management-a-core-theme-in-management-research-and-education-conference-arnoud-franken-14-june-2016-sheffield (accessed August 20, 2020).

Gasik, S. 2007. "Knowledge Oriented Project Management." http://sybena.pl/dokumenty/IPMA-knowledge-oriented-project-management-Gasik%20V1.2.pdf (accessed November 30, 2020).

Joshi, K. 2001. "A Framework to Study Knowledge Management Behaviors During Decision Making." In *Proceedings of the 34th Annual Hawaii International Conference on System Sciences* (hicss-34), Vol. 4.

Merchant, K.A., and W. Van der Stede. 2003. *Management Control Systems: Performance Measurement, Evaluation and Incentives*. Financial Times/Prentice-Hall.

Moravec, J. 2013. *Knowmad Society*. Minneapolis: Education Futures LLC.

Muslihat, D. 2018. "Agile Methodology: An Overview the Art of Iterative and Incremental Software Development." https://medium.com/zenkit/agile-methodology-an-overview-7c7e3b398c3d (accessed August 20, 2020).

Nielsen, J. 1993. *Usability Engineering.* Boston: Academic Press.

OGC. 2005. *Managing Successful Projects with PRINCE2.* London: The Stationary Office (TSO).

OGC. 2006. *Portfolio, Programme & Project Management Maturity Model (P3M3)* (Version 1.0). Office of Government Commerce (OGC). Crown.

OGC. 2009. *Managing Successful Projects with PRINCE2.* London: The Stationary Office (TSO).

Onna, M., and A. Koning. 2002. *De kleine prince2, gids voor projectmanagement.* Den Haag: Ten Hagen Stam Uitgevers.

Project Management Institute. 2013. *A Guide to the Project Management Body of Knowledge,* (PMBOK guide) 5th ed. Newton Square, PA: Project Management Institute.

Project Management Institute. 2017. *A Guide to the Project Management Body of Knowledge* (PMBOK guide) 6th ed. Newton Square, PA: Project Management Institute.

Rosinski, L. 2019. *Knowledge Management for Project Excellence.* London, U.K.: New York: Routledge.

Scheper, W. 2002. *Business IT Alignment: oplossing voor de productiviteitsparadox.* Information Science. Utrecht University, Utrecht.

Schindler, M., and M. Eppler. 2003. "Harvesting Project Knowledge: A Review of Projectlearning Methods and Success Factors." *International Journal of Project Management* 21, no. 3, pp. 219–228.

Siles, R. 2020. "Definition of Project Success." https://pm4dev.com/pm4dev-blog/entry/definition-of-project-success.html (accessed August 20, 2020).

Turner, N.W., H. Maylor, L. Lee-Kelley, T. Brady, E. Kutsch, and S. Carver. 2014. "Ambidexterity and Knowledge Strategy in Major Projects: A Framework and Illustrative Case Study." *Project Management Journal* 45, no. 5, pp. 44–55.

Weerd, I. 2006. *Meta-Modeling Technique.* Draft for the course method engineering 05/06.

Weick, K.E., and F. Westley. 1996. "Organizational Learning: Affirming an Oxymoron." In *Handbook of Organization Studies,* eds. Clegg, S.R., Hardy, C., and Nord, W.R., 440–458. London: Sage.

Williams, T. 2004. "Identifying the Hard Lessons from Projects Easily." *International Journal of Project Management* 22, no. 4, pp. 273–279.

Wikipedia. 2020. "RISMAN." https://nl.wikipedia.org/wiki/RISMAN (accessed August 20, 2020).

Zaleznik, A. 1993. "Leiden managen: een belangrijk verschil." In *Organisaties op de divan - gedrag en verandering van organisaties in klinisch perspectief,* ed. de Vries, K, 97–114. Scriptum Books, Schiedam.

About the Author

Lukasz Rosinski has a bachelor's degree in information sciences and a master's degree in business informatics from Utrecht University. He is the creator of three management frameworks: Projects with Learning Outcomes (ProwLO), HybridP3M, and The Progressive PMO, based on a book trilogy. Lukasz is the founder of CyberKnowmad and owner of platforms such as KnowledgePlace (a document management system for projects) and Insight Intranet.

Index